IN A

BRETON STEW

by

David Brewer

Published by

Mabel and Stanley Publishing – March 2025

For Kerry, Jack, Harry, and Maggie.

Special thanks to Kerry for all her help and encouragement, and for giving me that extra nudge to get this book over the finish line.

As far as I can remember, this is a true story.

Chapter One

We all stood on the drive and waved off the removal lorry. We, being my wife Kerry, eldest Jack, who would have been 12 years old, Harry 10 years old, Maggie 7 and me, Dave. It was July 25th, 2002, it was a beautiful summer's day. The driver stuck his head out of the window as he pulled away, and shouted, "See you tomorrow." The kids yelled back "See you in France." As the lorry rounded the corner and was gone from view, we all looked at each other. I wondered as I looked round, were we all thinking the same thing. What are we doing? What have we done? Will we be alright? Will we want to come back in a month's time? Will we ever see our furniture again?

I guess we were all thinking something like that. Well, all except Maggie, who seemed more concerned about her dollies and teddy's, especially her power puff girls spending the night in a cardboard box, in the back of a big smelly lorry.

Well, this was it, the big day had arrived, we were leaving England behind and moving to a big old stone cottage in the middle of the Brittany countryside in France.

We turned around and went back indoors, it was empty inside apart from a cage with the three guinea pigs, Tony, Jake and Dexter, the aptly named Birdy the budgie sitting on her swing in her cage, and a cat carrier box within which lay Dodger, the big tabby tomcat, who unhappy with his situation was moaning a lot. The only thing we were leaving, was a fancy leather sun lounger, this was to be my chair and bed on trips back to the UK until the house was sold.

We loaded up the car with our little menagerie and said goodbye to the house. The strangely named Horseradish Hollow, in the village of Hoo, had been good to us. It had been a bit of a dump when we moved in, but this was reflected in the price, and it gave us an opportunity to afford a house in Hoo and get out of our first house where we had never been completely happy. Over two or three years we had worked hard and managed to turn the house around into somewhere where we were proud to live. The house was in a stand-alone block of three, we had lovely neighbours both sides. We knew we would become friends with them, as not long after we moved in, Harry came indoors munching on a hot dog. When asked where he got it from, he told us it was from next door, they were having a BBQ. Water fights between the neighbours and the boys became a regular thing. Despite being happy with where we lived, my work was proving difficult both mentally and financially, a long-standing contract that I was running ended abruptly. The boys had their challenges at school and were both having a tough time. So, after a house meeting over dinner one evening, we all agreed it was time for a change. We decided on a new adventure, we were moving to Brittany.

To find out how we came to be in a position of being able to move to Brittany, you have to go back nearly a year to September 2001. We were looking forward to a family holiday in Florida, doing the whole Disney theme park thing. When the terrible events of 9/11 happened, you couldn't help but be affected by those terrifying images that were screened around the world. We were no exception and getting on a plane to fly to America didn't seem the right thing to do. The holiday was cancelled, and we did our best to forget about it and carry on. A week or so later, a note was dropped through our letterbox, it was from an old friend. The note said, sorry I haven't been in touch lately, here's my new phone number, give us a call, from Bernie. Now, it was Bernie, who a couple of years previous, had taken me on my first trip to Brittany. I called him up and while chatting, I asked him if he still had his house in France. "Yes of course," he said, an idea quickly formed in my head. "Would you mind if we stayed there for a week?" I explained, about our cancelled holiday and that we were looking for an alternative. He said it wouldn't be a problem to stay there for a week and could we give him a lift down with us, as he hadn't been there for a while, and he could show us around.

The October half term came, and we found ourselves at Bernie's cottage in the heart of the Breton countryside. It was Kerry and the kids first trip here and they were proper taken with the place. The beautiful countryside, the tranquillity, The wood burner and the smell of wood smoke, the livestock, and the smell of cow shit. In time, driving down to here, we were to recognise the smell of woodsmoke and cow shit, as a sign we were getting closer to home. After a couple of days and over a glass of wine, I ventured the question: you know houses are quite cheap here, shall we have a look around and see what's out there. As we talked about it, Bernie, overhearing our conversation, told us that his mum, Joyce, had a house, albeit a renovation project, nearby that she was looking to sell. Curious we went to see the house and it was love at first sight. It was a typical Breton farmhouse with metre thick stone walls, a traditional slate roof and inside oak beams and two large fireplaces. The roof was in good nick as were the walls, the windows, and the doors. It was secure and watertight. It had a septic tank and the plumbing, and electrics had been started. The kitchen, a large room basically consisted of a sink propped up by a couple of sticks. As we looked around the property and excitedly talked things over, we became aware that the majority of the renovation works were all inside. All projects, that between us we were more than capable of carrying out ourselves.

In the interest of being sensible, we did look at some other properties, some amounted to just a couple of gable ends filled up with stinging nettles and brambles, they were a good price though. Despite looking at these other houses, our heart was set on Bernie's mums' house.

A couple of days before we were due to travel home, we met up with Joyce and made an offer on her house. She accepted and the next day after some arrangements being hastily made, we were at the Notaires office, signing documents. We also found ourselves writing a cheque from our British bank account in Francs. Kerry had spoken to the bank that morning, told them of our plan and surprisingly they said they would honour the cheque. As we left the office Kerry said, "most people when they go on holiday bring back a stick of rock but oh no, not us, we have to buy a house."

As we walked across the car park Joyce turns to us and said, "well seeing how you have paid the deposit the house is as good as yours, here have the keys." That way if we wanted to come down and get any work done, while waiting for the final signature day we could. The final signature day we learnt, was to be in three months' time, apparently this is the norm, as the property must go on some sort of agricultural list to make sure local farmers don't have a problem or objections to the sale taking place.

We spent the last days of our holiday at our new house, making plans, changing them, and making new ones. Taking photos, doing drawings, and making more plans. But even before this holiday and the buying of the house, to find out where the idea came from and why this part of France. We will have to go back two or three more years. I'm not sure where the original thought came from, it's something I've always fancied doing. And the idea was nurtured by a clerk of the works, at a job I worked on in Gillingham. At the time, this clerk was going through the process of renovating a barn, somewhere in the middle of nowhere in the French countryside. The barn was a full renovation project, and he used to spend all his holidays working there. He had many tales to tell and painted a lovely picture of rural life in France. At any given opportunity, I would swing the conversation round to his French property gaining knowledge from his experiences. It was something I dreamt of doing but didn't know if it would ever become a reality.

In time fate was to lend a helping hand, during the nineties I had a small building company in partnership with my brother-in-law, Martin. One day a Carpenter called Bernie came to work for us. That's it you've got it; it was that, Bernie. It was only after a couple of weeks of working for us, that he happened to drop into conversation, that he had a house in France. Suddenly Bernie was my new best friend, and it wasn't long before a trip down to his place in Brittany was arranged and Martin fancied coming along too.

The day of the trip came and the three of us travelled down to Portsmouth. It was a dreadful journey, torrential rain and high winds added together to make poor visibility for Martin, who was driving. It didn't bode well for our night crossing, across the channel to Saint Malo. The journey to Portsmouth was a slow trudge and we made it to the port just in time to catch our boat. Once on board, we dumped our bags in our cabin and like any self-respecting lads on a fact-finding trip to another country, headed straight for the bar. The ferry left Portsmouth and bumpily made its way past the Isle of Wight. Due to the conditions my mobile phone had not been cooperating on the drive down to keep Kerry posted on our progress. On the ferry, wasn't proving to be any more successful, I wandered all over the boat trying to pick up a signal. The only place I could find one was on the helicopter deck! I leant into the wind until I was able to clamp my arms around the handrail. I held on for dear life and dialled the number. I couldn't hear much above the wind, and the tables, chairs and other phone users being blown around. I got the gist of the conversation it was a bit of a bollocking for leaving it late to call. And no! said Kerry, Hurricane Edna wasn't an excuse. I made my peace, said my goodbyes, and returned to the bar. Unsurprisingly it became a bit of a session. Our time was spent, between the main bar where some half ass magician was trying his best to thrill the audience. And the piano bar where the pianist was happy to play our requests and have us sing along. It was a good thing the bars closed at 1:00 in the morning, as I think we would have stayed there all night, but the friendly bar staff threw us out. We somehow, wandering through the labyrinth of corridors, managed to find our cabin, climbed into our bunks, and slipped into a coma. While we slept, outside the elements conspired to try and tip the boat over.

In the morning, we were woken from our drunken slumber by music being piped over the tannoy system. This music, which was to become familiar to us over our years of travelling on the ferry, reminded us of a bunch of wandering mediaeval minstrels. The music was interrupted by an announcement telling us we would soon be arriving in St Malo and that breakfast was being served, so please get up now. Apart, for some reason, Martin walking up the corridor butt naked to retrieve his underwear, the rest of the crossing was uneventful. Even the weather had calmed down. Leaving the port, Bernie had suggested it was probably better if he drove, as Brittany was his second home, he knew the way and as well as that, he was more experienced driving on the wrong side of the road. We left the town of St Malo, and he promptly drove the wrong way, later after getting a bit of stick he was to blame his faux pas on the fog. We eventually made it to Bernie’s house but sadly realised we didn't care where we were, we had the mother of all hangovers and still had our sea legs. This condition seemed to worsen throughout the day, so much so, this first day of our trip paled into insignificance, and we all had an early night.

We woke the next morning, feeling refreshed and considerably more aware of our surroundings. As we stood outside drinking our tea, Bernie told us this was a typical autumnal Breton morning, there was no wind, just plenty of mist lying at its heaviest, over the ponds and low-lying areas. The trees, plants and grass were all heavy with dew and there was that smell, the whiff of wood smoke and cow shit, hanging in the air. As I stood there taking it all in, it occurred to me how quiet it was. There was no traffic noise, no machine hum, no aeroplane noise, just nothing, apart from the odd cow giving it large in the distance.

After breakfast and with the mist clearing, we set off to do what we had come here to do and look at some houses. I will always remember the first house we looked at. It was a large, detached stone property surrounded by

a garden, I say garden it was more like three football pitches. It had good walls, a sound roof and mud floors. It had a doorway, a very ornate stone doorway but no door. It had holes where windows should be and there was a massive fireplace at one end and above us massive oak beams straddled the walls to create the first floor, had there been any flooring present. It stood on its own in this vast field with just cows for company.
“This is lovely” I said.
“Yes, and it can be yours for the sum of 8,000 of your English pounds” replied Bernie.
We moved on looking at more houses, barns and longeres. Some had roofs, some needed repairs to the roof, and some didn't have a roof at all. Some were in a reasonable state of repair, while others just amounted to a pile of stones with a tree in the middle. We first timers were loving it, the fresh air, the smells, the quaint little Hamlets, and little villages we passed through.

Our appetites well and truly whetted, it was lunchtime and time for something to eat. We stopped at a restaurant that Bernie told us was the equivalent of a transport café. Using Bernie’s mastery of the French language, neither of us ended up with the meal we wanted but it was lovely food, all five courses of it, supplemented with wine and brandy. After feasting for a couple of hours, we settled the bill and headed off back to Bernie’s house. Now, Bernie’s mum lived permanently in Brittany, in fact she lived next door to his house. He said on the drive back that we really ought to pop in and see her, he hadn't seen her for a while and after all she was only next door. Arriving back, we went up to her door, Bernie knocked and let himself in, beckoning us to follow him. Bernie's mum, Joyce, was pleased to see us and before we could tell her about the mighty fine meal we had just had. She announced, dinner will be in about an hour, you boys must be starving, I have done a nice roast with all the trimmings. We didn't have the heart to tell her we had just eaten, so not wishing to hurt her feelings we kept quiet. Luckily, Joyce had a dog, and it was coming up to walkies time, we volunteered our services to take the dog out, in the vain hope, a bit of exercise would mean we could walk off some of our dinner. We tried to make the walk as energetic as possible, there was even a futile attempt to climb 30 foot up a tree to collect some mistletoe. At dinner we managed to eat enough not to cause offence, and it was only after the table was cleared and more glasses of wine drunk, did Bernie spill the beans and tell his mum about our dinner experience earlier that afternoon. The evening finished off back round Bernie's house sitting in front of the log fire, drinking red wine, discussing the day's activities, and generally talking bollocks.

Well, that was my first trip to Brittany, and in that short time it had made quite an impact on me. So anyway, back to where we were.

After signing the first lot of paperwork, paying the deposit, and taking ownership of the keys. Our next trip over as a family was to be during the upcoming Christmas holidays. But first, leaving the kids with my mum, Kerry, and myself, did a quick trip down to the house at the beginning of December. We felt we needed to do this to sort out a few safety issues, get the house looking a bit Christmassy and organise some logs for the fire. The safety issues were little things like the big hole on the first floor, where the stairs had once been. And exposed electrical wires, sharp edges, and general builders' mess. We managed to achieve this in two days, and we were soon back home looking forward to our Christmas break.

The standout memory from that trip at Christmas is bedtime, Kerry and I slept on a sofa bed, while the kids all had camp beds. The house with no furniture no heating, no nothing really was extremely cold. All we had was an open fire, so the beds were in a half circle around the fire, with everyone's feet at the warm end. The kids all went to bed nigh on fully clothed complete with gloves, woolly hats and in Harry's case a fetching balaclava. The memory I have is them all lying in bed dressed like that, reading their comics.

We came down to Brittany the following February, paid the balance and signed the final papers. The house was officially ours. We were blessed with lovely weather that February and ate our lunch outside most days, using an ironing board as a table and whatever we could find to sit on as chairs. We really needed to sort some furniture out.

Chapter Two

The fun begins…...

Home was now a small hamlet called Treblou in the heart of the Brittany countryside. I realised after a couple of days that an anagram of Treblou is Trouble, Should I have heeded the warning signs, who knows? Our nearest village was called Guilliers and was about 5 minutes' drive away. For a small village it had plenty of amenities, a baker's providing fresh baked bread and delicious cakes, there mille feuille was legendary. And still is. There was a butcher, that was linked to a local farm where I'm sure if you wanted to, you could go up the field and choose your cow. Opposite the bakers was a small supermarket called 8 till 8, that opened at 9am and closed at 6 in the evening! Never could work that one out. The village was also the home of a small primary school, where Maggie and Harry were soon to go. There was also the obligatory tabac and three other bars. The centrepiece in the village square was the 12th century church, surrounded by 5 roads shooting off in different directions, lined with houses that looked like they'd been drawn by Disney for the film The Aristocats. Guilliers was situated between the village of Meneac and the small town of Mauron, maniac and moron – another sign?

Maniac and moron actually came true when we met a couple who lived not far from us in Treblou. I shall call them Rose, who was the maniac and Fred the moron. We had heard only bad things about them, but we were prepared to give them a chance. It turned out they owned quite a good chunk of Treblou, a very long Longere consisting of three houses, complete with large gardens and an orchard. Over the road from them they also owned a large meadow with a pond in the corner. The way they carried on, you would have thought they owned half of France. They started off friendly enough, but their advice usually turned out to be completely wrong. We never went out shopping on a Monday, to start with, because we were under the impression that all the shops were closed, based on what Fred, and Rose had told us. Turns out it was just the bakers and the small supermarket in Guilliers that were closed on a Monday, everywhere else was open as usual.

Before we moved to Treblou permanently, Rose had taken a dislike to a couple of trees, in our front garden and wanted to cut them down. As she didn't want the leaves in her garden. It seemed a bit nit-picky to want our trees cut down considering her garden was surrounded by trees, and particularly the woodland bordering her garden on the other side. So, we politely declined her offer. On our next trip down, we pulled up onto our front garden to be greeted by two eight-foot stumps, the trees had been proper massacred and there they were, no branches just 8-foot stumps. I was a bit cross and was all for going straight round to see Fred and Rose and have it out with them. Kerry calmed me down and we decided ignoring them was the best policy. Before we left for home from that trip, I made a sign saying, "Private Property" and hung it from one of the trees. The next trip down revealed that the sign had gone, and it was like Rose had been lying in wait for us. She suddenly appeared and was very animated, she had great pleasure in telling us that she had seen the sign, gone and got a broom and knocked it down. We later found the sign behind the log stack. Rose was an intimidating kind of person, and she would spend most of the day shouting at people, mainly Fred, but more often than not the varied tradesman and gardeners who had the misfortune to work for her. She would often shout at me over the fence, that she needed me to come round and now, not in ten minutes! I ignored her.

The other neighbours in the hamlet, that is the French neighbours, had no time for her either, or if her name came up in conversation, it would usually end up in that time honoured French traditional gesture of showing disgust. The action involved putting your left hand into the middle of your right arm, then bending the right arm, while blowing raspberries. This action was finished off with a resounding "Salop," which as far as I'm aware isn't a very pleasant way of describing someone.

Now, although Fred was complicit in the madness, he was mainly harmless. He seemed to spend most of his days in some sort of trance, we were to learn later from Rose herself, that she would often up his pill dosage, especially when he stepped out of line and was a bit cheeky to her. Apparently, he was on all kinds of pills, for one thing or another. His lumberjack abilities were not top of his skill set, and anyway whoever thought it was a good idea, to let him loose with a chainsaw, is anyone's guess. One afternoon he took it on himself to cut down a medium size oak tree on the edge of their meadow. He started off making the V cuts, so far so good. Then he thinks maybe it would be better to go up the tree and cut some of the branches off. So up he goes and then what follows must have been like some scene from an old cartoon. He sits on a branch and begins cutting the branch but it's the wrong side from where he's sitting. Before he spots his deliberate mistake, the branch gives way and Fred, chainsaw and branch end up in the Meadow. It could have been a lot worse, and he is fortunate to come out of it with just a broken arm. We get to hear about the story because Rose comes up that evening and tells us all about it and demands that we come down now to the meadow to finish off the job, as she's worried that the tree could fall into the road. We had just got ready to go out for the evening and we had dressed smartly for the occasion. We explained this to Rose and said I'm sure the tree will be fine till the morning and then we will come down and finish the job then. But Rose, as I have said, can be quite intimidating and very insistent and despite our protests, 10 minutes later, there we were, down the meadow to finish cutting the tree down. There was no time to get changed, I found myself operating the chainsaw while Kerry looking resplendent in her little red miniskirt outfit and high heels hung on to a rope. Rose of course took the supervisors role and hollered instructions, Fred appeared, looked on sheepishly and stood there saying nothing. The job done; salt was rubbed into the wound when a car with some of the locals in, went by shouting abuse, about the cutting down of a decent oak tree. I could possibly write more about what these two got up to, but I'll leave it there. There was much relief from the hamlet when after two years of us moving there, they moved back to the UK. There was even talk they were on the run because of some benefit fraud.

Our closest neighbours were Rene and Edith, a typical salt of the earth Breton couple, who I would have said were both in their 80s. It took a little while to strike up a friendly relationship with them; to be fair, they probably judged all English to be like Fred and Rose. Rene first came to our attention, with his routine of leaving home every morning at 7 o'clock, to visit the tabac in the village for his newspaper and glass of pastis. His garage was about 50 metres from our house but every morning, especially if we were still in bed with the window open, we would brace ourselves for what was coming. We would hear the door slam shut on his ancient Renault 5 and then a minute or so later the car would be started. The engine would be turned over three or four times before it burst into life, and then know sooner had it done that, Rene's foot would go hard down on the accelerator. That poor car would have the guts revved out of it for what seemed like an age but was probably 3 or 4 minutes. When Rene thought the car was good and warmed up, he would reverse out of his garage. On most days he would bump into a large flowerpot on the corner of his drive. Perhaps, I should have offered to help move the pot at some time. He told me once that his eyes were bad and that he probably shouldn't be driving, but living where we did there wasn't any other option. There were no buses here to hop onto. Most of the roads in the Brittany countryside had ditches on either side, so Renes' driving technique, to avoid ending up in a ditch, was to drive down the middle of the road. If anytime we noticed Renes' car was missing from his garage, we tried to avoid driving out if we could help it.

I got to experience he's driving first hand, when one afternoon he asked me if I would mind helping him move a TV set. "Of course, No problem" I said. He led me into his house and made his way up the stairs. The stairs were very old, very creaky, very steep, and very narrow. We went into what was obviously his bedroom and there on a chest of drawers was a massive 50-inch-wide TV, which was as deep as it was wide. No luxury of a light flat screen TV here. I wondered to myself how the TV had got here in the first place; Rene beckoned me over. He was signalling for us to take an end each, which we did and began making our way to the top of the stairs. Somehow, we were making our way down, there was lots of puffing and panting and I began to feel as if, I was carrying the TV and Rene too. This was the first time I heard the expression "Zut Alors" Rene said it quite a lot. I think the literal meaning is damn then. Amazingly the TV made its way into the back of Renes' car, I breathed a sigh of relief and made to move off back home. But before I could leave, Rene asked me if I would accompany him to Guilliers to help him out with the TV there. Before my brain could engage with what had been said, I found myself agreeing and getting into the car. I fumbled for the seat belt and checked it had engaged several times before I was content it was secure. As he went through his usual start up procedure, I tried to convince myself it would be fine, after all, he does this journey every day. We reversed out, bumping into the long-suffering flowerpot as usual and carried on down the lane. At the bottom of the lane, he managed to stop smoothly at the give way sign. OK, I thought to myself that wasn't too bad, perhaps I've been worrying unnecessarily. Although no sooner had that thought entered my head when Rene suddenly rammed the gear stick into first and wheel spun down the road to Guilliers. He quickly sped through the gears, and we were soon moving along at quite a lick and as previously reported, in the middle of the road. The road to Guilliers has quite a few bends and as we negotiated one of these, there on the road, coming towards us, was a cyclist, I tried to call out a warning, but nothing came out. Rene oblivious to the hazard carried on, leaving the cyclist no option but to take evasive action and do a bit of off roading, through the foliage on the verge. As we got through the bends and entered the last straight towards the village, my worst fears were realised, when coming towards us was a car. I thought about closing my eyes, I even thought about opening the door, jumping out and taking my chances in the ditch. But there I sat transfixed like a rabbit in headlights. As the car got closer it started flashing its lights and beeping its horn, but like Rene chose not to slow down. Somehow, we missed each other, the only casualties were a section of stinging nettles on the verge, a lot of which ended up wrapped around Rene's wing mirror. We arrived at Guilliers with no further excitement and unloaded the telly. Thankfully, the journey back wasn't as dramatic, as we managed the drive home without encountering any other road users. We pulled onto his drive bumping into the flowerpot for good measure and got out of the car.

"Merci beaucoup," said Rene.
"No problem, anytime" I lied.

Rene and Edith had their routines, one of them being, their afternoon walk or promenade. At dead on 3:00 PM they would leave their house and start on their circular walk around the hamlet and fields, a journey of approximately 3 kilometres. It didn't take long for Rene to take the lead, and they would do most of the walk with Edith walking some 30 paces behind. One afternoon we were sitting in our front garden and noticed Rene return on his own, nothing unusual there. He waited by his front door then went back out to the lane and looked up the hill. Seeing there was no Edith in sight, he began to get animated and upset. We made our way over to him and he told us that he had lost Edith, she was nowhere in sight, and he just assumed, she was following him as normal. We called the kids up and quickly formed a small search party and retraced the route they always take. Edith was soon found, when her legs were spotted sticking out of the cornfield, she had stumbled, lost her balance, and fell into the corn and had been unable to get up. Despite her calls, Rene hadn't heard her and had carried on walking. Edith was a little shaken, so we helped her home and reunited her with Rene. We went back to our seats in the garden and was treated to Edith giving Rene some verbal's for the next hour.

It was thanks to Rene and Edith that we experienced our first proper aperitifs event. Rene came round one afternoon and after the usual formalities' handshakes, kisses, and small talk he explained the reason for his visit. Our French was still very limited at this time, and he seemed to be asking after our staircase. But after a few gestures some miming and pointing it dawned on us that he wanted to borrow our ladder. I got the ladder out and asked him where he wanted it and what he wanted it for. He told me that he needed to clean his gutter out and led me to the offending gutter in question. I positioned the ladder and despite Rene's protests I climbed up. I couldn't stand by and watch an eighty plus year old gent climb up my ladder, I wouldn't have forgiven myself had he have fallen off. The gutter wasn't that bad and was soon cleaned out. As I was putting the ladder away Rene was full of thanks and said he would sort something out for me. I told him not to worry, it was no problem, after all, that's what neighbours do for each other.

After I'd been back home for about five minutes, there was a knock at the door and there stood Edith. Again, after the kissing and small talk she invited us round to their house tomorrow evening for aperitifs," Children to come too" she said, leaving no room for discussion. That will cheer them up I thought. Kerry enquired as to what time they wanted us.
"Well 5 o' clock, of course" said Edith "when else would you have aperitifs".

The next day duly arrived and at precisely 5 o'clock we knocked their front door. Rene opened the door and invited us in. The greetings and kisses seemed to go on forever, we had now moved up the social ladder and were on four kisses terms now, amazing what a bit of gutter clearing can do to improve your social standing. I could never understand the etiquette of the kiss greeting, sometimes it could be one but more often than not it was two, rarely three and here we were now on four. Someone told me once, that as a rule of thumb, there is no rule of thumb. In the case of a man greeting a lady, the man should take the lead from what the lady does. I tried to adopt this and was often left hanging with me, kissing air, and displaying an expectant cheek. This kissing greeting lark took a further twist when French male chums, that I had known for a while and had become good friends with, started kissing me. It was only on the cheeks thankfully but was a strange custom to get used to.

Rene ushered us to our seats and the kids were provided with orange juice and peanuts. Once they had been sorted, Rene turned to Kerry and me and asked what we would like to drink. The choices were pastis of course, porto, whisky, and malibu. I still wasn't a massive fan of pastis, I have never really been into aniseed, even as a child I didn't like aniseed sweets. I wasn't sure about the porto. The malibu seemed to have some sort of culture experiment growing around the lid. I'm not a great whisky drinker either, I'll have a glass or two over Christmas and New Year's Eve but that's about it. Decision made, I chose the whisky and a half pint tumbler three parts full, was handed over. There was probably more whiskey in that glass, than I had drunk in the last two years. Kerry, obviously not noticing the culture experiment, chose the malibu but to be fair the lid did get a wipe with a damp tea towel. Rene poured himself a small pastis and Edith had a glass of water. Cheers! or Yec'hed mat! – the Breton for cheers was the call and we all raised our glasses. Now for the small talk, the weather was of course the first topic on the agenda. They say us Brits are obsessed by the weather but the locals around these parts weren't far behind. The children were invited into the conversation, and they were asked how school was going. They did join in even if it was one-word answers. I had the impression that they would rather have been anywhere else then sitting here this particular evening but then I could have been wrong! The conversation moved on to the annoying neighbourhood barking dog, the equally annoying Parisians that had just moved into the hamlet and then their favourite subject, Fred and Rose. The mere mention of their names was accompanied with gestures and the blowing of raspberries, oh, and they were still Salop's!

As the conversation sort of flowed, I started to take in the surroundings. Their lounge was a busy room with traditional carved wooden Breton furniture, there were photos and paintings covering nearly every inch of wall space. The content of the pictures suggested to me that someone had obviously travelled a lot. The pictures were mainly of African origin, brightly coloured sunsets, Savannah scenes and a variety of African animals in various poses. Rene spotting me studying his pictures explained they were from his time when he worked in Africa, mainly Algeria. I wondered if this is where he had picked up his habit of mowing the grass in his Y fronts. Mind you, cutting the grass in a state of undress wasn't uncommon in Treblou, Francoise who lived down the lane from Rene and Edith enjoyed cutting the grass in the nude, whilst riding her sit on mower. This caused a minor commotion amongst the small population of Treblou, well especially the male population. Who on a balmy summers' afternoon, hearing the sound of

Francoise's sit on mower starting up, would feel the need to take the dog for a walk.

Anyway, back to the aperitifs and Rene was explaining how he had spent time in the military and in the police force, he had been in Africa because of his work. The ornaments and trinkets that were all over the room followed the same African theme. Although in amongst them were some strange surprises, there were bald barbie dolls, barbies with various limbs missing, a my little pony with a rather harsh skinhead haircut, and dolls and teddies in various states of disrepair, arms, legs even heads missing. I was beginning to think I have seen these before and Maggie confirmed my suspicions when she caught my eye and mouthed, "they are my toys." Now, Edith was no cat burglar, but she was very adept and agile when it came to diving in the communal waste wheelie bin. It wasn't unusual to drive down the lane past the wheelie bin to see Edith's bum sticking out of the bin and her little legs dangling off the ground. Many the time I've called out bonjour, to Edith's bum, to get a reply echoing from the depths of the bin.

While this was going on I had somehow managed to drink all my whisky, and Rene, despite my protests had filled my glass up again. Kerry had been quite good and had only been taking little sips of her drink. She told me later she hadn't noticed the mould on the lid of the malibu bottle until after she had asked for it, but then didn't want to cause offence by bringing it to their attention.

Rene started to tell us of his exploits during the war and his part in the Resistance. I am surprised the Nazis managed to stay in France, for as long as they did, as nearly every old boy we had spoken to, was in the

Resistance. The majority of the old boys, you took their stories with a pinch of salt but there were no such doubts with Rene, his seriousness when talking about his exploits and his army and police career all backed it up. We were to find out in time that Rene was highly thought of and well respected by the people of this area.

Listening to Rene telling us his stories of his interesting life, I had only gone and drunk the second glass of whisky. Rene took the empty glass and me feeling no pain at all encouraged him to fill it up, much to Kerry and the kid's annoyance. Although Kerry despite her small sips, had finished her glass too, and had to endure another glass of malibu. The wonders of alcohol had improved my French remarkably, well so I thought. I had started to slur but wibbled on regardless. Kerry, backed up by the kids started to make, it's time to go, noises. But being in full flow and enjoying myself I finished off the third glass. Kerry spotting an opportunity and before the glass could be replenished stood up and said it's time we were going. I slowly stood up on my now rubbery legs, which went some way to remind me, just how much whisky I had drunk. We said our goodbyes, with lots of kissing and embracing, and left. Outside the fresh air hit me, thank heavens we didn't have far to walk. We had been out for about two hours, and all that whisky in such a short time had an effect. As my eyes became squinty to the point of shutting, I thought to myself, so that's aperitifs eh! I could get used to that. And with that I promptly put myself to bed.

Chapter Three

It was a lovely sunny summer's afternoon; The kids were all on their school holidays and we were on our way to cut the grass at a friend's house that wasn't too far away. The house was an old derelict place that had cost next to nothing, it had no services such as water and was a full renovation project. It also had a massive garden that needed a lot of work, mowing etc just to keep on top of it. The journey from our house to here was a short drive along a single track so the kids were all sitting in the trailer with the gardening equipment. As we approached the hamlet which consists of seven houses, five of them in a row and the other two detached and in prominent positions. Rounding the bend the houses came into sight, and on a lawned area we noticed a long table had been set up and around the table was seated a dozen or so people. As we passed by, the kids waved and cheered, and the party goers responded the same. We carried on around the back of the property to enter the garden. All the garden was around the back there was no front garden as such. We started unloading the equipment and designating jobs, when suddenly through the undergrowth, we were joined by one of the party goers. Being one of the neighbours he knew of us because of our efforts to maintain this garden. He was also aware that we were English and because he spoke a bit of English he had been elected to come round and invite us for a drink. He explained that the reason for their get together was that once a year the residents of the hamlet came together for food, drinks, and a catch up. He said they would very much like it if we would come and join them. We replied that, we needed to do the garden first and then we would be more than happy to accept the invitation. He said he looked forward to seeing us soon and disappeared back into the undergrowth.

We all got stuck into the gardening and soon had it finished, we loaded up the trailer and made our way round the front to join the revellers. As we approached the table there was much cheering and everyone got up to greet us. We were treated like long lost friends, there was much handshaking, embracing and of course the obligatory kissing. We were invited to sit down on chairs, that looked like they had been freshly plucked from one of the houses. We were told this little bit of garden existed solely for the purpose of this get together. The table was lavishly laid out with mouth-watering pastries and cakes, and plenty of alcohol. There were bottles of wine and champagne nestling in ice buckets, the condensation running down the bottles and glistening in the sunlight, made them look very desirable. We were told to help ourselves to food, while Kerry and I were passed generous glasses of wine. The kids were handed glasses of lemonade and plates of cakes.

As I sipped on my glass of wine, I took a moment to look at all the guests gathered around the table. It dawned on me, that from the young man who had invited us to this gathering, to the elderly gent, who appeared to be struggling with the laws of gravity, that, they were all rather drunk. After the disruption of our arrival, the laughter and conversation quickly resumed, gathering pace it was soon in full swing. But now, we were the centre of attention and were being asked a lot of questions. The questions were the usual stuff like, where had we lived in England? How long have we lived in France? Why did we come here? Like I say, the usual stuff. Until one of the guests, a fella probably in his late 50s, not particularly scruffy but not really smart either, he had a mousy face and was sporting one of them moustaches that seem very popular with his generation around these parts. He was also very over refreshed.

"Avez vous un Chatte" he asked, turning to Kerry and placing a strange but strong emphasis on the T. There was, stifled giggling around the table.
"Oui" replied Kerry, the giggling turned to laughter.
"Est-ce que un belle Chatte" the fella said, lapping up the plaudits from his audience.
"Oui, C'est Grande et poilu et s'appel Monty," said Kerry.

Well, that was that! the table erupted and not wishing to be left out we sort of joined in. While this uproar was going on, Jack seized the opportunity to lean over to Kerry and myself to explain the reason for their reaction. He told us the fellow wasn't asking after your cat he was being rude and talking about your pussy. We had a quick French lesson in which Jack told us that cat in French is Chat, but you don't say the T. Now Chatte means pussy, but you have to emphasise the T. As the mystery was explained to us and the penny dropped, our laughter increased and so did our hosts. After a while things started to calm down, apart from the odd sigh and gasp for breath. Relative silence broke out as everyone composed themselves, but this was only to last for a few moments, when one of the old boys shuffling on his seat let out a thunderous fart. We were off again, more laughter and when this subsided the fartee did the gentlemanly thing and blamed his wife. The laughter was interrupted by more drinks being served and cakes being passed around.

Glasses and plates topped up, things settle down for a bit, just general small talk broke out around the table.

Until that is Monsieur "Pussy" directed his attention to Kerry once again and asked her if she would like French lessons.
"Oh yes" said Kerry, "anything to improve my French."
Mr Pussy went on, this was all being done in French by the way.
"Ok I will do you a deal" he said" I will give you French lessons and in return you can sleep with me."
The laughter ramped up a gear and was accompanied with feverish table banging.
Monsieur Pussy, well and truly in the chair, carried on.
"Do not be worried that your husband will be cross, he can sleep with my wife" and with this he pointed to the frowning embarrassed woman sitting next to him.

And then it was champagne time, corks were popped and sent flying in all directions. Everyone, including the children, were given a glass and then began a round of toasts.
"To our family and neighbours, Cheers"
"To our friends, Cheers"
"To our new English friends, Cheers"
"To the countryside and our lovely hamlet, Cheers"
"To this beautiful weather, Cheers"
"To Jean-Pauls thunderous fart, Cheers"

Suddenly the toasts were interrupted by a crash and a small scream of distress, the old guy had finally lost his battle with gravity and disappeared under the table. There was a brief pause and then someone shouted.
"What are you doing, it's too early to be looking for mushrooms."
More uncontrolled laughter followed, and the old guys head appeared at the table, he reminded me of how Captain Mainwaring of Dads Army fame looked, after one of his tumbles. His face, all red and his hat and

glasses at a skewed angle. The old guy was sporting a small cut on his forehead, which was dealt with by dipping a napkin in some champagne and being held on the wound.

This scene of fun and laughter carried on for about another hour, then it was time for us to go. We said our goodbyes, like we had known them forever, the warmest of handshakes, genuine friendly hugs, and kisses. One of the women even shed a tear, we had gone from complete strangers to good friends, in a couple of hours, what an afternoon.

Chapter Four

One evening I was having a quiet beer and several noisy ones with my good pal Eddie; amongst our waffling, we decided we would meet up every Sunday morning at 9:00 AM, outside the boulangerie, in Guilliers and go for a bike ride. Come rain or shine that's exactly what we did. Sometimes Jack would join us and about once a year Harry, would grace us with an appearance. As I said we would go out in all weathers - rain, blisteringly hot, freezing cold, thick fog and even snow. An average Sunday morning would see us complete about 50 kilometres. It was a great way of keeping fit and exploring the back roads and trails of the Brittany countryside. Now and again, we would even see a car. It also became a great hangover cure, no matter how late we had got in, on the previous Saturday night or how much we had had to drink, we were always there. Although feeling pretty rough when we started the bike ride, we somehow rode through it and by the time we had finished, our heads were clear, and we were ready to start again.

These rides usually passed off without incident, we had both managed to part company with our bikes at some time, due to black ice, frost, or a rogue cowpat. Eddie one time had a disagreement with an electric fence, he had grabbed it with both hands to prove it wasn't live and ended up, dancing about like some sort of performing marionette. Jack was with us that particular day and couldn't stop laughing. He was still laughing weeks later and couldn't look Eddie in the eye without cracking up. Occasionally some old boys, from one of the many local cycling clubs, resplendent in there brightly coloured Lycra, would latch onto us and use us as their pace setters. We would of course take this as a challenge and try to shake them off, but we seldom did. And after a while, bored with us, they would bid us "Merci," pick up the pace, overtake us and speed off into the distance. Leaving us feeling a tad dejected. Now and again, we would get lost but that was about it, we were just a couple of lads out on a Sunday morning bike ride joking about and sharing some banter.

Until one Sunday morning…...

The alarm went off at about 8:00 AM, and I awoke to a beautiful summers' morning. As I went downstairs, I called out to Jack, "are you joining us this morning?" There was a slight delay and then back came the answer "yeah OK." There was the normal routine of having a cup of tea and swallowing a banana. The bikes were then checked over, tyre pressures, brakes etc. Happy with the checks, we set off. There are two ways of getting into Guilliers by bicycle, one is the usual road route that we would take by car. The other is to follow the farmers tractor trail between the fields and the woods. As we went down the lane, I said to Jack.
"What way shall we go today."
"Let's do the tractor track" he replied.
To take the track we had to pass by the row of 17th century cottages, that we affectionately had named Treblou High Street. Once past these we were on the track, mainly woodland to our left and fields to our right. After about one kilometre the track, hits a crossroads, still a tractor trail but to the left we would skirt the woodland and to the right we would pass between two fields, our route today was to go straight on. As we passed through, Jack, looked up to the left and shouted.
"Hold on Dad, there's a scooter lying on the track."

And with that he changed direction, to have a better look. As he got closer, he yelled out again.
"Dad come quickly; there's someone lying next to it."
I turned towards him expecting to be disturbing some unfortunate drunk that had come off his scooter and was sleeping it off. As I approached the scene there was a scooter still looking quite new and shiny lying on its left-hand side and next to it was its former passenger, lying face down in the dust, his positioning straight away suggested that he was quite dead.
"Err, is he alright," said Jack.
"No, I don't think so" I replied, "he looks very stiff, and I would say quite dead."
Rigor mortis had already set in.
"Oh right" said Jack calmly, as if this was an everyday occurrence.
Thinking what to do, I said to Jack, "I'll stay here, you are going to have to nip home, explain to mum what we have found and where, and that she needs to call the gendarmes."
I watched Jack cycle off and disappear around the corner, I turned round and looked at the poor unfortunate fella lying on the track. He was beginning to look familiar, like I should know him.

Kerry was still in bed when Jack burst in through the front door doing his best Corporal Jones impression,
"Don't panic, don't panic everyone, we've found a dead body, don't panic" he shouted.
Kerry hearing the commotion came running down the stairs and tried to calm Jack down, so as to learn the facts.
"We have found a dead person; he was lying next to his scooter along the track," said Jack." You have got to call the gendarmes; dad has stayed with him, and I've got to get back."

Jack blurted out some rough directions and with that he left as quickly as he had arrived, to make his way back to the scene. He was joined by Harry who had been woken by all the commotion, and who was not usually aware this time on a Sunday morning existed.
"Jack, did you say you found a dead man?" shouted Harry, getting his bike out of the shed.
"Yes" replied Jack.
"Bloody hell" said Harry, "I'm coming too."
So, some 15 minutes after Jack had left me, I was joined by both Jack and Harry.
"What are you doing here" I said to Harry.
"I don't know really!" replied Harry" I think I wanted to see what a dead person looks like."

It was over 20 minutes before we had heard a siren, it was getting closer and closer and then further and further away. And then there it was again, getting closer and closer and then further and further away.
"They can't find us," said Jack.
We heard the siren again but this time we could make out the blue flashing lights. We jumped up and down and waved our arms in the direction of the flashing lights but to no avail, it sped off into the distance. This could be a long day I thought to myself.
"We need a plan" I said "Jack, you go up to the top of the hill until you hit the tarmac road and wait there, Harry you go the other way until you hit the road, and you wait there too. Hopefully, the gendarmes will drive by, and you can direct them to me, here."

Once they were stationed on their designated roads, the plan soon worked and down along the track came Jack, followed by a fire truck bristling with Pompiers (firefighters). I was surprised to see it was a fire engine that was the first emergency vehicle to attend. Where was

the fire? The truck skidded dramatically to a halt and outjumped a pompier with a large first aid bag over her shoulder and started to run towards the body.
"I don't think there is any need to run" I said.
Ignoring me the pompier passed by me and knelt by the poor unfortunate soul lying on the floor. Realising his condition, she shouted out to her fellow pompiers, who were breaking out the resuscitation equipment,
"Don't worry about that, he's dead."

The urgency gone out of the situation, the pompiers relaxed and gathered around the body lying on the track. They started asking us questions and told us that the gendarmes would be here shortly. While we were talking a mobile phone rang, it was coming from the dead guy's trouser pocket. There was a bit of head scratching, everyone looked at each other for a moment, wondering who was going to take the lead and answer the phone. As one of the pompiers took the initiative and leant forward to take the phone, it stopped ringing. That could have been an anxious wife or family member, not sure how that conversation would have gone. We heard a siren again, and this followed the now familiar pattern of getting closer and closer and then further away. One of the pompiers got on the walkie-talkie, called up the gendarmes and they were soon with us. They joined the circle and asked if it was us who had found him. They quizzed us for a bit and said we would have to go to the police station this afternoon to make a statement.

Then there was another siren but this time they come straight to us, mind you we were starting to stick out a bit now. There was quite a crowd of us, and a selection of vehicles gathered on this lonely track. The latest people to join us were paramedics, who despite the body looking very grey and with rigour mortis definitely set in,

they began the routine of checking for a pulse, feeling for a breath and then check on the heart with a stethoscope. Finally satisfied, one of them pronounced the poor fellow dead.
The paramedics stood up and joined the discussion circle. The chatting was disturbed by the sound of another vehicle coming along the track. It stopped, and out got the lady who runs the local timber yard. She went round the circle, shaking hands and kissing some people who she was obviously familiar with, as if this was some kind of social gathering. I was wondering why she was here, was it to take measurements for his coffin! As the kissing and handshaking came to an end, she finally turned her attention to the reason why we were all standing here. Amongst the "ooh la la's" while talking, she explained to us, the reason for her presence, was because she was the deputy Mayor, and it was normal for someone from the mayors to attend such situations.

And then there was a sound of another vehicle approaching, I turned round to see the commune maintenance van, very dignified I thought taking the body away in that! The driver got out of the van, approached our group, and went round us all, shaking hands. He then looked at the poor feller on the ground and joined in with the "ooh la la's." The van driver then explained, his reason for being there, he had seen all the vehicles and the small crowd and was just being plain nosy.

After a while, the gendarmes told Jack, Harry, and me that we could go but don't forget to come to the station this afternoon to make a statement.

When I got home, I thought I better ring Eddie to tell him my reason for not showing up for the bike ride this

morning. After I had explained the whole story, his reply was.
"A couple of hours late and that's the best you could come up with."

Kerry went into Guilliers, to pick up our Sunday morning bread, news had travelled fast! and we, were the talk of the village. Kerry wasn't allowed to leave the shop until she had told one and all what she knew.

It turned out that the chap who had died, was the same fella that we referred to as 'Monsieur Pussy' at that garden party we'd had such a good time at. Poor man. In time we were to find out that he had a serious heart condition, was on medication and really shouldn't have been drinking.

When sometime later, I was talking to Eddie about this whole episode, I happened to mention that if I ever get round to writing my book, I will definitely have to include this story. He suggested that if I was giving chapters specific names, I should call this one "A morning stiffy."

Chapter Five

After about 18 months of working on the house, Kerry taking French lessons and otherwise loafing about in the garden drinking beer. It was decided that it was time to look for work, our savings wouldn't last forever. Being a carpenter, it seemed the obvious route was to set up a carpentry business. People were always telling us there was plenty of work for tradesman in the building game in this part of the world. We spoke to a friend in the local bar one day about our plans and he said our first port of call should be the Hotel de Impot - the tax office. They should be able to advise and put us on the right path to setting up a business - or so our friend thought. Our nearest tax office was in Ploermel, our nearest town about 15 kilometres away. After dropping the kids off to school one Friday morning, feeling brave we headed off to Ploermel and the tax office. Once in the town centre the building was surprisingly easy to find, it was a typical French government building, with the French flag - the Tricolour, the flag of Brittany - the Gwenn-ha-du (which means white and black in Breton) and the EU flag all fluttering in the wind outside the main entrance. We entered the building and as we approached the reception desk, I bravely shoved Kerry in front of me to deal with the nice receptionist man. Kerry explained the purpose of our visit and after a couple of attempts he got the gist of what she was trying to say and directed us to the first-floor, room 7. With a sigh of relief, we thanked him and made our way up to the first floor. The door to room 7 was open so we went in and there was another reception desk, we approached the desk and once again Kerry explained the reason for our visit. The lady behind the counter understood straight away but told us that we didn't need this room, you need room 12. So, with new directions in our heads, we made our way to our new destination and some more explaining. This time there was some serious head shaking and discussions between members of staff who eventually concluded that what we were after could be best resolved on the next floor up in room 16. We were beginning to think that this was some sort of wind-up French farce. Nevertheless, we made our way up on to the next floor in our quest for room 16. We knocked on the door and a female voice beckoned us in.

Once inside, the room was smaller than our other office visits. This one had just the one desk behind which sat an elegantly dressed woman, in front of the desk were two empty chairs. The woman stood up and welcomed us in with bonjours and handshakes. We sat down and we explained ourselves again, well at least Kerry did. After the explanation, worryingly we had the same furrowed brow, the look of puzzlement and head shaking that we had experienced in our previous office visits.

"Excuse me, one moment" she said, and left the room.

She was gone about 10 minutes but when she came back in and sat down, she was smiling and seemed to have an answer for us.

"So just to make it clear" she said, "you are a carpenter, you would like to be self-employed and set up your own business."

"Yes, that's it" said Kerry, we were starting to feel like we were getting somewhere.

"Ah" she replied, "you need the Chambre de Metiers."

The Chambre de Metiers, is a bit like our chamber of commerce dealing mainly with small businesses.

So not only were we in the wrong room, which had happened several times, we were in the wrong building!

We left the building, crossed the road, found a bar, and ordered a couple of beers. Over these beers it was decided to leave the Chambre de Metiers adventure till after the weekend. The road to setting up a new business in France had not had the best of starts.

The following Monday, after dropping the kids off at school, we found ourselves once again heading off to Ploermel, this time to visit the Chambre de Metiers. Finding the building we pulled into an empty car park and our suspicions were confirmed when as we approached the door, we spied a sign saying, "Closed Mondays." But the same sign also read open Tuesday till Friday. Hopefully, we wouldn't lose our motivation and would try again tomorrow. Motivation not lost; we did try again on the Tuesday. The car park this time showed signs of life, and the entrance door had a sign proudly proclaiming that they were open. We went up to reception and explained to the studious looking woman behind the desk, the reason for us being there. We were getting pretty good at it now after Friday's practise runs. The lady understood why we were there and said,
"This is the right place to set up a small business, but first, seeing how you are a "étranger" (foreigner or stranger) you will need to get your trade and qualifications recognised in France."
She went on to explain that this could be achieved by going to the prefectures office in Vannes. You will need to take proof of trade and qualifications, and any other documents, photos etc that might help your cause. You will have an interview at the same time. She gave us the necessary contact details and address and wished us good luck. We made our way home; the process had begun - well almost.

Once home Kerry rang the prefectures office and an appointment was made for two weeks' time. We were to learn from this phone call that there was only one chap in the whole of the department of Morbihan, who was responsible for recognising people's qualifications and trade, and thus giving them the green light to proceed with their business plans. Let's hope he is a nice man.

Two weeks passed quickly, and we make the journey of about an hour down to Vannes. We found the office pretty much in the centre of town, it was a massive imposing gothic type of building, and in we went. There was a large information board just inside the main entrance, we located the office we required and made our way there. We reached what we thought was our office and the sign on the door confirmed this. We entered and was confronted with a scene that looked like an old bank. There were wooden panelled counters with ornate patterned glass screens, in the screens there were half-moon holes that we used for talking and passing things through. The staff, all ladies that were working these counters looked quite the serious type, we chose the least scary looking one and approached the counter. We explained the purpose of our visit, in that we had an appointment with Monsieur Trade recognising man. There seemed to be some hesitancy and uncertainty once we'd explained why we were there, and there was much glancing at the door on the right.
“If you could wait a moment” she said, “I need to talk to my supervisor.”
She disappeared over to the desks at the back of the office and began talking and pointing at us and that door on the right. The lady who she was talking to got up from her seat and they both came over. The new lady introduced herself, as the supervisor and said unfortunately Monsieur trade recognising man, couldn't

see us today. But, we said, why is that? we have booked an appointment, we need this appointment to be able to start work and it's taken us an hour's drive to get here.
"I'm sorry" she replied "but Monsieur will be seeing no one today" with again more strange glances at this door on the right.
What was going on?
We had a few more attempts that pleading our case but realising we were getting nowhere and ultimately not wishing to cause a scene - we left.

That evening Kerry rang her French teacher and told her what had happened. The teacher agreed that it all sounded a bit strange and said she would ring them up for us tomorrow, to find out what's going on. She rang us back the next day and told us it wasn't our fault, we had got the date and time right, but Monsieur Trade Recognising Man, had been taken ill that very morning, in fact it was happening while we were there. He was having some sort of episode and was threatening to throw himself off his office window ledge. The prefectures office said they had our details and would contact us when the Monsieur was all better.

Time went by; in fact, three months' time went by. When at last the Prefectures, office called and gave us a new appointment. A week or so later we were knocking on that very door that had been the centre of attention on our last visit. We were invited into what look like a dusty old headmaster's study. The Monsieur stood up and greeted us with a warmish bonjour and a handshake. He was an unassuming type of guy, he was short, grey haired, wearing little round glasses perched on a glowing red nose. So, the red nose, had that been the cause of the problem on our first visit, was he partial to the odd glass or two as his rosy hooter would suggest.

So began our plea, to get my qualifications and trade recognised. First up were the deeds of my apprenticeship, having served my time in a naval dockyard this was rather fancy. It was a large document with smart calligraphy writing and a rather impressive M.O.D wax seal. Then came my certificate of craftsmanship, this was more like a hardback passport. It had the Navy bases crest emblazoned on the front; very impressive I thought to myself as I handed the documents over.
"Very nice" he said, "but we don't recognise these qualifications here in France."

Undeterred I pressed on, next came business cards, headed notepaper, old invoices, tax returns, and VAT returns. He looked at them graciously, but nothing was appearing to tick that all important box yet. I fumbled in my case; it was a nice leather attaché case, that I had rescued out of the loft thinking it would make me look the part; first impressions and all that. Back to fumbling in the case, I found in one of the sleeves my old subcontractors' certificates. These were like credit cards but with my photo ID, National Insurance number and tax reference number. I handed them over and Kerry explained what they were. He studied them one by one and showed them a lot more interest. And then raising his eyebrows he looked up at us and said,
"C'est bon" and spun his chair round to face his computer.
Kerry and I looked at each other and smiled, I think we've done it.
He asked for some details, the usual stuff, full name, date of birth, address etc. He pressed the print button and from the copier in the corner of the room, out popped an impressive looking certificate booklet. He retrieved the booklet, signed it, dated it, stamped it, and handed it

over. It was official, my trade had been recognised, and I could now work in France as a carpenter.

Step one complete, we had the certificate, now what?

A few days later we were back at the Chambre de Metiers proudly presenting my very new proof of qualification certificate, to the same studious woman we had seen before. Everything seemed to be in order. She looked at me and said.
"Ah Menuisier, C'est bon"
Menuisier is a general carpenter, charpentier is a roofing carpenter.
She explained to us our next step in the process of setting up our business, was to go on a business management course. This course was aimed specifically at small businesses. Kerry asked if this was really necessary as we have run a business for many years. Sorry but it's the law in France for people setting up a business she replied.
"But my French isn't very good," I said, in my not very good French.
It doesn't matter, the law is the law, was the comeback.

The Ploermel office only did one of these courses a year and that had just gone. So, we were booked into the Pontivy office for three weeks' time, Pontivy was about an hour's drive away.

"How will you be paying for the course," said the woman.
"What! We must pay for it too" we exclaimed.
"Oh Yes, 350 euros for me and if I wanted Kerry to come to help out with the French language that would be another 100 euros!" we were told.
450 euros for a course, we didn't need and probably wouldn't understand most of anyway. So here we were,

some months after starting out, to set up a business; still not being able to work and a few hundred euros out of pocket.

Three weeks passed and there we were at 9:00 AM, on a Monday morning, sitting in a large classroom at the Chambre de Metiers office in Pontivy. It was a large featureless room with drab décor and not even any pictures to study during periods of boredom. The classroom was laid out with the desks around the perimeter of the room, the sides facing towards each other and the back row facing the front. At the front there was a desk, a large TV screen and a lectern. Everyone was seated and a quick tally up revealed there were 22 of us and they all looked as cheesed off as I felt. The door opened and in walked our lecturer, she looked like she was in her mid-twenties, she was smartly dressed, and I thought, reasonably attractive. Although her attractiveness waned as the week dragged on, due to her monotonous tone of speech and her curious mannerisms. She approached the lectern and introduced herself, which I observed received a muted response. She then asked, that we go round the room, introducing ourselves and stating the nature of our business. There was quite a cross section, from hairdressers to gardeners, from mechanics to those in the building trade.

Day one started off boring, was a bit boring in the middle and ended off boring. The only thing to come out of this day, was to understand that our lecturer, loved the sound of her own voice. She also did annoying things with her arms and hands while speaking, it was if she was the signalman landing a jet on an aircraft carrier. As the first day was coming to an end, she cheered us all up by letting us know if we missed a day or were even late, we would have to do the whole course again. After the day was finished, we approached the lecturer and asked her if there would be a test at the end as we were a bit concerned about my French not being up to scratch. She told us there wasn't a test at the end and if your French really isn't that good just sit there and try to look interested!

Day two was just as boring as day one. Although there was some minor excitement when a guest speaker turned up. He was the manager of a local bank but unfortunately proved to be just as dull as our beloved lecturer. He did show us a film, in which a scruffy man, with his paperwork in a carrier bag, goes to the bank to ask for a loan but is turned down. Then along comes a smartly dressed man, he's carrying his documents in a nice shiny attaché case and surprise surprise, he gets his loan. This was about as exciting as this course got.

To stop myself having dark thoughts of throwing myself out of the window, I began compiling lists. I started off with Beatles songs, then moved on to Disney films. I was quite impressed with my list of Clint Eastwood films; of just how many he had done and that I could remember them.

Day three got off to its usual dull start, and looking around, it was starting to tell, you could see on the students faces and by their body language, that they were starting to have had enough. This was underlined that afternoon, when a group of students who had been out and had lunch together, clearly, they had had a glass of wine or two and started to get a bit lively. When the lecturer began her usual droning monologue, they started asking questions and even began arguing with her. Saying the course was a waste of time, money and was very boring. I had not got a problem with that, all true as far as I was concerned. Not letting up, they said their time would have been better spent out earning rather than sitting here - again very true. The lecturer gamely tried to defend the courses' role in the scheme of things, but she was no match for her wine fuelled antagonists.

The lists were going well today, the big contenders were Elvis Presley songs and Tom Cruise films.

Day four, losing the will to live, as is I think everyone here today. Not the lecturer though, she is still enjoying herself, as she waffles on and on and on. I'm surprised she doesn't take off when waving her arms around like she does. Another special treat we have our second guest speaker, but where do they get these people from, yet another exponent of the art of being a dull dreary twit. I wasn't really sure what his speciality was or what the point of him being here today was. But thinking about it, I don't think anyone else did or cared for that matter. His lecture over ran and passed our finishing time, everyone was getting fidgety, coughing, and hinting at the clock on the wall. But this is when Kerry hit hero status amongst her fellow students, she calmly stood up and announced that time was up, and we had children to pick up and had to leave. And with that we left, followed out of the room by the rest of the students leaving a bemused guest speaker staring after us.

At last day 5. I had done my best fill up my pad with these random lists, but I had run out of things to make lists about. It became a case of just counting down the minutes, I started counting things like bricks in the wall, tiles in the ceiling and leaves on the tree outside the window. I did a snap survey on the colour of peoples socks, sitting opposite, it came with its own little burst of excitement when I noticed one of the guys opposite had odd socks on. I don't think I can cope much longer. Our lecturer plodded on and on and on. It seemed like a deliberate quest to bore the complete arse off us. Lunchtime came and we decided to treat ourselves to a "Plat du Jour" at a nearby restaurant. The meal came with wine, which amounted to a couple of healthy glasses each. When we got back to the classroom it seemed most of the other students had all had the same idea. The atmosphere was definitely feisty. The afternoon was spent with the more vocal of the group arguing with the lecturer about the relevance of the course. At last, the hours turned to minutes and then it was home time. We had made it! We were hoping to leave with the necessary paperwork so we could crack on and finally get some work. But we were told the paperwork would be put in the post and we should have it within a week.

Two weeks later; the paperwork arrived.
With our new paperwork and a small amount of confidence we set off once again to the Chambre de Metiers office in Ploermel. Upon our arrival we were seen by youngish guy who seemed a lot happier than our previous interviewers. He found our file and checked everything over meticulously while we sat there staring on nervously. After a while he looked up and told us, everything looks in order and your business is now registered, you just need to sign some more forms. He pressed a button on his computer and the printer started spewing out a long line of paperwork. The paper just kept coming and coming and after what seemed like an age it came to a stop. After much signing, God only knows what we were signing, we were done.
Our interviewer, rose from his seat and said,
"That's it, you are now legal to start your business, good luck."

He offered us his hand, which we shook warmly, we thanked him and made our way to the nearest bar.

We definitely deserved a beer it had been a long road, it had taken six months, cost us over €600 but at last we were there, we were registered to work.

Now all we had to do; was find some work.

Chapter Six

So began the process of trying to find some work. We put adverts in expat papers and magazines and also on expat websites. I sharpened up my chisels and waited for the calls to start coming in.

In the meantime, bureaucracy hadn't quite finished with us yet. We had several people come to visit us to get us to sign up for, what we were in time to call the dreaded "cotistations." This is like the UK's National Insurance, but is broken into three parts, health, pension and general other stuff like Social Security, welfare payments etc. These visitors we're all officious humourless suit types who were just keen to get our signatures for their companies cover. This was obligatory and we had to sign up for the cover even before we had done a stroke of work and earned a penny. We were told that the cost wouldn't be so bad in the first year but would rise each year with the fourth year becoming the most expensive. Four years seemed a long way off so dutifully we signed up.

After a few weeks, the inquiries started to come in and we won our first job. It was for a lovely couple who had moved to Brittany from Goa. They had bought a house in the High Street of a small town and wanted to turn it into an Indian restaurant. The house needed a lot of work, walls taken down, new stud work built, lots of plaster boarding and general carpentry. A price was agreed, and we soon started work. A lesson that we learnt in the first week was not to go to a restaurant every lunchtime for a "plat du jour." A "plat du jour" is the meal of the day, it's usually a set menu, consisting of three to five courses and usually comes with cider or wine. So, after filling our stomachs and having a glass of wine, the motivation and enthusiasm wasn't at its strongest in the afternoons. We decided on having one "plat du Jour" a week, and that was to be on a Friday, we would have our lunch and finish early. Problem solved.

The work went well, and the clients proved to be a delightful couple to work for. The smells that came from their kitchen were just delicious and we were often called on to taste the latest dish that they were working on. A lovely perk of the job, I suppose.

Work picked up through advertising and more satisfying through word of mouth. It appeared doing our first job at the restaurant had been a shrewd career move. The open day saw many people turn up, probably enticed by the offer of free food. But for us it proved to be a good networking event, we met other trades and picked their brains for information and advice, potential customers, and an accountant.

We were pricing up lots of work and were doing something right, as we were winning most of them. Generally, everyone we worked for were really nice people. There is always the odd idiot, like the woman who when we were working on her staircase wouldn't let us take our tools inside, because they might be dirty. Not sure how she thought we were going to get the work done. These types of people aside, most of our clients became good friends. We were often invited over for dinner or just drinks after we had finished the job. We worked on all sorts of projects, from a small job lasting a day to a full renovation running for two to three months. Some of these jobs were lovely old buildings, in beautiful locations. One that sticks out was an old railway building in a siding by a single line railway track.

There used to be one train a day, that used to go chugging by and the driver was always happy to blow his whistle and give us a wave. On the other side of the building was a track, that led to the client's houses and behind them was a canal. The clients were two couples, they were very friendly and very understanding and appreciative of the problems, that were faced on such a large renovation. Most days they would sit outside their house and eat their lunch, and most days they would invite us over to join them. They usually laid out a vast buffet type spread, baguettes, cheeses, cold meats, salad etc, all washed down with large quantities of wine. Not particularly good when you're hoping to crack on with your work in the afternoon. One day, Kerry had prepared a large pot of breakfast pasta for our lunch, the pot consisted of pasta, eggs, beans, sausage, and bacon. When we had our invitation over to lunch we took the pot with us. Kerry took the lid off, plopped it on the table, and said help yourself. Well, help themselves they did, they ignored their own spread, kept exclaiming how wonderful it was and between them ate the lot.

The work took just over two months to complete, and they were so happy with what we had achieved, they took us out for dinner. We often visited them long after the works was completed and became good friends.

It became the norm, although not taken for granted, that the client whose house we were working on, would invite us to join them for lunch. And of course, with wine. One customer cooked us a rather large roast dinner followed by apple crumble and custard for pudding. I struggled to get up the ladder that afternoon.

I could probably count on one hand the clients we had problems with, I'd like to think I'm a good judge of character. I could often smell trouble when we met a prospective client for the first time to price the job up. If I thought that they could be a problem, I either went in with a high price or didn't bother pricing it up at all. On that "one hand" of problem clients, it includes small things, like the time I took Jack with me, so he could help me with some lifting and the clearing up, and at the same time earn himself some pocket money. With the job finished I asked him to tidy up, clear the rubbish and have a good sweep up, while I went off to sort the final payment out with the client. When I came back, Jack had removed all the black sticky tape from the floor, that had been carefully measured and placed down by the client, showing him where units were to be located. The client wasn't best pleased and really didn't see the funny side.

The worst client we had, and it still remains a mystery as to why he turned like he did. He was an ex-copper, and I'll shall refer to him as PC Git, not that I'm angry about how he treated me or anything like that. He first contacted me by telephone and was very near to tears as he described what had happened to him, his property, and the predicament he now found himself in. Apparently, he had let this builder loose on his house, who as it happened turned out he didn't have a clue as to what he was doing. The final straw came when PC Git, found the builder who had hidden himself away, and was reading the Reader's Digest book of DIY as a way of getting help. They had a row and PC Git gave the builder the boot. I agreed to meet up at his house and when I got there the property was indeed a mess. Lots of things started but not finished, there were holes everywhere, bits of ceilings and walls missing, windows and doors poorly installed and the plumbing and electrics were all messed up. It was quite a challenge.

I called up an electrician that I had met, at the Indian restaurant open day. I told him all about the job and he agreed to come on it with me. We started a couple of weeks later and began putting the house right. We concentrated on the jobs, that would have had a health and safety officer pulling his hair out, as to the state the property had been left in. After all, the clients were still living in the house while the work went on. We decided to leave the kitchen to last as that was a massive project on its own. In time and a lot of hard graft, the rest of the house was duly finished, and PC Gits wife was so happy with how we had turned things around. Work started on the kitchen which included knocking a wall down that the previous builder insisted couldn't be done. The wall came down, we made good and fitted a new ceiling, then new windows and doors. As the kitchen neared completion, the tears of despair from PC Gits wife turned to tears of happiness. However, it was noticed that there was a change in mood in PC Git, he became a bit frosty and abrupt, not sure why! Anyway, the job was finished, the result was one extremely happy PC Gits wife but one not so happy PC Git. Perhaps he suspected the sparky of having an affair with his wife, who knows? We had no idea why his mood had changed. Life goes on and the sparky and I left the job congratulating ourselves on a job well done.

A few months later with the job long forgotten, an anonymous thread appeared on one of the more popular expats websites. The thread went on to slag off an electrician and a builder who had done some work at his house. To me it was obvious who he was referring to because he had picked phrases that we had both used on our advertisements. I contacted the website to complain, that the comments were untrue and could cause damage to both our businesses. The website that was famed for deleting posts at the drop of a hat refused my request. Messages of support started appearing on the thread and eventually the post was removed. Before it was removed, I had managed to find out who had posted the message, by replying to it privately, it took you to a link, that revealed the website for the bed and breakfast run by PC Git. I emailed him and asked why he had posted it, at first, he denied it was anything to do with him. But when I told him of what I had done and how it followed the link that led to him. He eventually admitted it, but I still couldn't get out of him as to why he had done it. All he would say, was that he had had too much to drink one evening, and that it was the wine talking. My offer of a face to face meet up was politely refused, what a git!

To this day I still don't know what his problem was, we rescued him from a desperate situation, turned the job round, carried out what I thought was great work. His wife was extremely happy and so was he until the last couple of days. His drunken rant on that website could have done untold damage to our future work prospects. What a complete git!

While doing our renovation works, we would often be asked if we knew anyone who could carry out garden maintenance like cutting the grass. Realising there was another business opportunity, we set up a garden maintenance service with Kerry at the helm. This worked both ways, as we got gardening work, while carrying out renovation projects, and renovation work, while carrying out gardening. Soon this part of the business was as busy as the renovation side.

However, cutting peoples grass and looking after their gardens bought out new eccentricities that we didn't realise existed in people. There was one guy, who insisted we used his beat-up old mower. Even though ours was an all singing all dancing, top of the range lawnmower. His was old, non-self-propelled and unreliable. His grass had to be cut at the exact height of 2.5 inches and there wasn't to be a single grass cutting left. He had run a wire on some sticks, creating an area, that he would like mown, and we were under strict instructions that no cuttings must go out of the wired off area. He dispensed with our services when somehow, he found out that we had been using our own mower. Perhaps a neighbour had told him, but we weren't really bothered, who needs that sort of nonsense in your life.

Someone else who was particularly fussy and deserves a mention. A client of ours, who was an elderly lady, she was a painter, no sorry, an artiste! Kerry used to attend to her every need in the garden, and she was another one, who was particularly uptight about the height her grass was cut at. Our artiste was definitely from the luvvie school of art, she had had exhibitions, don't you know! Although the first time I went round there and saw some of her work, I thought my dog with a brush in his mouth could have done better.

Not only did the grass have to be of the right height, but there was also a particular pattern that had to be followed, and she watched over this with a critical eye. If Kerry was planting flowers for her, she was continually getting told off for putting them in the wrong place. "Not there dear" was the usual comment followed by instructions telling her to move the plant a half inch to the left.

One day while Kerry was gardening, I was there as well, as I had been roped into decorating the artiste's toilet. I was halfway through the first coat of emulsion, when the old girl appeared, and asked if I would mind vacating the room, so she could use the toilet. I left her to it and went into the garden to see how Kerry was doing. After a short while she reappeared, told me I could carry on and resumed barking out her instructions to Kerry. I returned to the toilet to carry on painting and was confronted by the most awful smell. The old girl had taken a shite, God knows what she had been eating. It could have been chemical warfare. I opened the window and retreated to the garden gasping for breath.

This leads me nicely onto why we drifted away from working for her. When we were there going about our jobs, she would insist on working with us and over us. The first time she tore one off, apart from a quick glance at one another, Kerry and I ignored it. Until the stench hit us, struggling for breath, we had to move away to avoid retching or even throwing up. No sooner had the smell subsided, she let another one go, this time with a bit more ferocity, she didn't try and conceal them, she just let them go. If you had the misfortune to be bending down, planting or weeding and she was standing there, she would make no effort to move. And "parp" you would get the full force. What could have been funny, was proving to be most unpleasant. We found ourselves at risk of losing our lunch, every time we experienced one of her bottom explosions. So, we started drifting away, we ignored her calls and requests to go round to work. There're not too many jobs I can say that we have given up on because of the customer's rancid arse.

As mentioned earlier in this chapter, one of the nicest discoveries when we started work was the restaurants serving a "plat du jour." The meal of the day consisting of three to five courses and anything from one glass of wine or cider to unlimited wine or cider. As mentioned, we stopped the practise of doing this daily and would only indulge on a Friday. We would finish mid-day, make our way to a restaurant, where we could eat, have a couple of glasses of wine and relax, knowing that was the start of the weekend. Being set menus we encountered some interesting dinners, cow tongue and chicken gizzards spring to mind. To be fair, they didn't taste as bad as they sounded but invariably ended up, with me finishing Kerry's dinner too.

In time we found ourselves a restaurant, that would become our favourite and every Friday despite where we were working, we would travel there to enjoy their hospitality and fare. The restaurant was situated on the edge of the massive Lanouee forest, in a village called Les Forges. It was so close to the forest, that one day while dining there, we were treated to the sight of a herd of deer grazing on the forest edge. The menu here was five courses with unlimited bread, water, red wine and or cider. The starter was usually a cold platter, something like a tuna potato salad. The second course was a hot savoury pastry. The third course was the main meal, meat or fish, potatoes or rice, and vegetables. This was complemented with a large bowl of lettuce drizzled over with a delicious garlic and shallot dressing. Then followed the cheese tray, A nice selection of cheeses with extra bread if required, delicious homemade bread at that. And all the while we were eating, the wine would be topped up accordingly. And finally, it would be the sweet course, we got to know it off by heart, as quoted to us by the waitress. The choices would be "glace, éclair, Paris Brest, Ille flotant, tarte aux pommes au fruit." I always had the tarte aux pommes while Kerry had either the glace or Isle Flotant. These puddings were a delicious way to finish off a lovely meal. It was two hours of simple but fine dining. When we started using this restaurant, in 2004, it cost just six euros each, about four pound in those days. It was such great value for money, especially as you were fit to burst, and on some occasions, due to the amount of wine consumed, was a bit wobbly. The first time we ate there, feeling a bit over refreshed from a glass or two of wine, it was agreed that it might be best, if we took a long stroll around the forest before driving home. The red wine was supplied to the restaurant direct, from a vineyard owned by a friend of the restaurant owner's family. We were introduced to the vineyard owner, who was eating there one time, when we had stopped off for lunch. The wine was good and very often hit the spot, but it had a little side effect. When you looked around the restaurant, you could tell who had been on the red wine, their faces were bright red.

The restaurant was also used by the local school for their school dinners. The children would arrive promptly at 12:00 midday and leave at exactly 12:45. We figured the school to be a primary school as the pupils ranged from a tiny tot to 10-year-old students. The seating arrangements were made, so that an older child, sat with a younger one, the older one was then in the position to help the younger one with their dinner. They were always well behaved and if the noise level was to rise, the teacher would bring them in to check with a shrill SSSSSHHHHH! And silence would return.

We ate there many times and never had a bad meal. Whether it was our regular Friday lunchtime treat or a trip out with the family or friends we were never disappointed. Great food and lovely people.

Chapter Seven

I was a regular visitor to the expat websites, they were a good source for work, things for sale and the latest gossip. I was particularly interested in a post, I saw one day from a guy from the BBC, on the discussion forum page. For the programme "Inside Out" they were doing a feature on people who had moved from France and set up a business in Kent and wanted to compare their experiences with someone who had moved from Kent and set up a business in France. Thinking that we fitted the bill I replied to the message, I gave a brief description of what we had been up to and left some contact details. That evening the phone rang and I found myself talking to a producer from the BBC. After a bit of a chat, a date was arranged, we said our goodbyes and hung up. We are going to be on the telly, I shouted, the BBC are coming to see us.

As the day loomed near, the house was cleaned top to bottom -several times. The dogs were bathed and so were the kids. It probably would be a good time to mention, that despite knowing that the BBC were coming, and that in all probability he would be on telly, Jack decided to dye his hair bright red. Looking like a swan vesta matchstick would certainly get him noticed.

For the filming, the kids were given the necessary time off school, the head teachers were very accommodating and even excited for them. It was a cold January day when the film crew turned up, there were three of them. Mike the producer and sound man, Mike the cameraman and Glen the presenter. We had been expecting Kaddy the usual presenter on Inside Out, but the two Mikes jokingly told us later that there had been unrest from the wives at the thought of them travelling away with Kaddy.

Introductions over, it was time to start filming the first scene. This was to involve Glenn walking up our lane, turning into our drive and meeting us at the gate. After the introductions we would invite him in. As I have already mentioned, it was a cold January day, something like -4°C, so we were hoping that this wasn't going to take long. Take 23 later and we were still going, dealing with lighting and sound issues and the dogs taking a shine to the cameraman. We finally got the opening scene in the can, as they say in the industry, and we went indoors for the next part of the feature. While Kerry and I were put through our paces with a rehearsal of the questions and answers, cameraman Mike took himself off around the house for some infill shots of the kids at rest and play, the wood burner and of course the dogs who seemed strangely interested and fond of him. Once we had had a few run throughs we were ready to go. The producer called action, he wasn't going to, but we asked him if he wouldn't mind, as part of the whole experience. The camera rolled and we were off, Kerry seemed to have developed this rather posh and refined accent for the filming. Time ticked on and several takes later we were still at it. There had been the usual lighting and sound issues and a few continuity problems especially when the dogs burst in and hassled Mike the cameraman again. Kerry and I had a few moments to ourselves, we weren't used to this kind of thing and a couple of times we even lost the ability to speak, and it was like our tongues had become a piece of wood. I think they call it "corpsing."

The interview rumbled on into the late evening, and after five hours of filming and talking we were getting a little bit thirsty. We were heavily into making our own homemade wine, so out came the Chateau Blackberry. The crew being very professional, turned the first offer of a glass down, but they soon agreed amongst themselves, it was only homemade what harm could it do. A couple of glasses later, they realised they had underestimated the power of the homemade brew. They made their excuses, blaming it on fatigue and called it a wrap. They said they would be back in the morning to continue filming for the feature.

Surprisingly, they arrived on our doorstep bright and breezy the next morning, they all said that their head felt a little fuzzy but again blamed it on fatigue. The producer told us they had been talking over breakfast and had come up with a great idea, that they wanted to run by us. They wanted to finish the piece off, in the village outside the "Maries" office, with me standing in front of it, wrapped in red ribbon, to symbolise red tape, which was miraculously produced from one of their bags. I took a little persuading as we still lived here after all and didn't want to upset anyone, especially the "Marie." And aside from that it was too bloody cold to be stood on a street corner wrapped in ribbon for too long. Offering reassurance they said that they would make it a quick shot. Off we went down to the village and just to make it a little more interesting the village market was on. Of course, it was a Tuesday and Tuesday was market day in Guilliers. It wasn't the biggest of markets, just a few stalls selling local produce of meat, veg, cheeses and the like. Not an excessively big market but nevertheless more people in the village square than there would normally be. Again, I expressed my concerns but was told" don't worry about it," as it will be all over before you know it.

In freezing conditions they began setting up their equipment, they decided they were going to use the tripod jib for the camera. The producer, Mike, took me to one side and said, it will be quite a simple shot, we will get you to stand there, pointing to a spot in front of the "Maries" building, Glen will come round the corner, you will have a brief conversation and then the camera will lift up and pan around, showing you standing outside the building. So, 20 minutes later, there I was standing outside the Maries office wrapped from head to toe in red ribbon and freezing my nuts off. The shoppers and stall holders at the market, had started to take an interest, as had anyone passing by in a vehicle. I was starting to feel a little uncomfortable and after the 17th take, a little tetchy. The cameraman, Mike, then announced he would like to put the extension on the boom to get a higher shot. Seeing my concern, I was assured once again that it wouldn't take long to set up.

I was bloody frozen, and a small crowd had gathered, muttering, and nodding amongst themselves as to why a strange man, wrapped in red ribbon, was being filmed in their Market Square, in Arctic conditions. It was something I had questioned myself more than once that morning.

Another 18 takes later and the crew finally agreed they had everything they needed, it was finished. The ribbon was removed, and I tried to move about to get some circulation going, in a vain bid to warm up. As I started to regain the feeling in my fingers and toes, I congratulated myself on the fact, that I hadn't been arrested.

We retreated to the local bar for a hot drink and something a little stronger. It was a "wrap" or "in the can" as us film types like to call it. The producer told us he would keep in touch and let us know when the programme would be coming out. He also promised to send over DVDs of all the filming they had carried out, over the last couple of days. We said our goodbyes and the crew left.

With the crew gone, the bar owner came over and asked us, what it had all been about. The filming and especially me standing there wrapped in red ribbon. We told him it was for the BBC and what the programme was about.
"But why the red ribbon" he asked.
We tried to explain, it was to do with paperwork and bureaucracy, an expression that we would use for this in England, is being wrapped in red tape.
"Red tape" he said, "It can only be an English expression, it's not something we would say in France" and with that he gave the traditional gallic shrug and went back to the bar.

So, my fear of being arrested or even put in the stocks and pelted with rotten food was unfounded. The bystanders or even the mayor, had he looked out the window would have had no idea what we were up to.

Chapter Eight

Once we were working and properly in the system, someone had mentioned that it was a good idea to register, with your local doctor and even make an appointment to meet them. We found out our local doctor was based in Guilliers. Kerry gave them a call and after a brief chat, we had an appointment booked for the two of us to meet the doctor and have a health check. It would appear we had just registered with the doctor.

Two days later with the appointment made for 8:00 AM, we got to the surgery 15 minutes early. The surgery was a modern building, located just off the village square; we entered the door into a hallway. Here was a small reception desk, behind which stood a small receptionist. She welcomed us in, and we explained our reason for being there and the time of our appointment. She ushered us into a small waiting room and said, "the doctor will call out your name when he is ready for you." The waiting room was approximately three metres by three metres with wooden chairs around the perimeter, and in one corner was a small table with some well-thumbed magazines piled on it. We sat down and acknowledged the other people in the room. There were two people already there, an old gent who looked like he was dropping in and out of sleep but still managed the strength to bid us Bonjour. And then there was a middle-aged lady who was totally absorbed in a magazine but still she managed to lift her head and gave a polite Bonjour. The waiting room had seating for 10 people, so it was nice and cosy and made the sharing of germs a little easier. The waiting room still had the smell of a recent decorating job, the smell of the builders magnolia paint still hung in the air. There wasn't much to admire in the way of soft furnishings, there was a vase on the windowsill with faded plastic flowers sitting in it. There was a picture with the sun setting over the sea on one of the walls, which was a bit scant on detail and didn't require a lot of studying.

In time more people came in, nodding to everyone as they sat down and wishing one and all bonjour. The two people, who were there before us, were called to their appointments, and just over an hour after we arrived, the door opened, and the doctor's voice called out our names. We were to learn that while you were given appointment times this was seen as a guideline, and it made sense to bring a book with you as it generally operated on a first come first seen basis. We were greeted at the door with a warm handshake by our doctor and welcomed in and asked to take a seat. The doctor was a short man, possibly late 50s with grey hair and wore glasses, the sort that you would expect a doctor to wear. He had a round friendly face and was wearing a tweed suit, which looked like it was made for comfort rather than style. He introduced himself as Doctor Jean and sat down behind his desk. His actual surgery was about three times the size of the reception area and waiting room combined. The centrepiece of the room was his vast antique oak desk and chair, behind which was a large bookcase full of thick leather-bound medical journals. The rest of the room had more traditional medical items, a reclining bed, a sink, scales and various machines, and owls. Yes, the room was full of owl ornaments, pictures, and cuddly toys. The doctor noticing us taking in all the owls, told us, that he loved owls and all the owl items we could see in his surgery, were gifts from grateful patients.

It was our turn to talk, and we introduced ourselves in our best well-rehearsed French and explained the reason

for our visit. Somehow, he saw through our accent and started talking in exceptionally good English. Again, he welcomed us to his surgery and said it was a good idea to come and see him, as he likes to get to know his new patients. He also said, he was happy to speak English, as he enjoyed speaking it and liked keeping in touch with the language, so he didn't lose it. He spoke to us for about 45 minutes, getting to know more about us, and I think he would have spoken for a lot longer, had the receptionist not buzzed through on the intercom; to remind him he did have other patients waiting to see him this morning.
"Oh well" he said, "I had better do some doctor stuff."

He then spent the next 20 minutes doing blood pressures, weighing us and that sort of thing. He then wrote us out a prescription to have a blood test, he told us we could get it done in Ploermel tomorrow morning, just turn up. He then went on to explain, that we would need to pay him €20 each, but with the help of a form, that he gave us, we could claim €18 back. We handed over the €40 in cash which he put in his pocket, no cash box here I thought. So, an hour after entering his room, he got up and made his way to the door and opened it for us. As we left, he shook our hands again and wished us good day. We walked out past the waiting room, to feel the icy stares of 10 thoroughly titted off prospective patients.

The next day was a Friday, so we decided to leave the trip into Ploermel and our blood tests till the Monday. Our weekends could be somewhat messy, on the party front, with plenty of booze and general overindulgence, so leaving the blood test until the Monday wasn't our smartest move.

On the Monday we made our way into Ploermel and parked in the town square. We found the clinic tucked away in the corner of the square. It was a modern glass fronted building with automatic sliding doors for the entrance. Just inside was the reception desk, we handed over our details and in less than 10 minutes we were all done. We were told we could pick up the results later that afternoon or alternatively they could be posted, and we will receive them tomorrow. We opted for the postal option and left.

The following day the yellow postal van turned up at 1:00 PM, as he did every day and there sure enough were our blood test results. We each opened our own results up and tried to study them, but to be honest these things are hard to understand in English, let alone French. Amongst all the long words, percentage signs and figures, there at the bottom of the page, on my results was written in block capitals surrounded by little stars, The word ** ALCOOL **. The after-effects of a sociable weekend were still in my system. That might raise an eyebrow at the doctor's, I thought.

A couple of days later, we were back in the doctor's surgery, to discuss our blood test results. He went through Kerrys first, her cholesterol was showing slightly high but nothing to worry about at this stage. Then he turned to mine, again cholesterol was showing high, but it was the word **ALCOOL** at the bottom of the page that caused the most interest. And as expected did raise an eyebrow or two.

"Do you drink much alcohol" asked the doctor.

"Yes, I do like to drink a bottle of wine with my dinner, as surely do all French folk" I replied hopefully. Thinking to myself this is France, who doesn't have a

bottle of wine with their dinner, but at the same time regretting choosing a Monday to have a blood test.
"The test has registered a high level of alcohol in your blood," said the doctor.
"Oh, really!" I replied, reminiscing of the vast amount of wine, I had drunk that previous weekend.
He then went on to say that we both needed to change our dietary habits and at one point talked at great length about a trout dish he enjoyed and how to cook it, and how good it would be for us. The cookery lesson went on for about 20 minutes or so and then he went on to discuss the evils of alcohol. He said one glass of red wine, was fine with your meal and he didn't mean one of those large glasses, that holds a whole bottle either. He chuckled as he said this, it would appear our doctor had a sense of humour. He carried on by saying he would give us a month to cut down on the cheese, butter etc – all the things that pushed up cholesterol. Also, we were to cut down on the booze and then do another blood test.

After a month of being good, a subsequent blood test still showed my cholesterol as being high. The alcohol reading was OK, mainly because I had had the presence of mind, this time, to lay off the booze a few days prior to the test. Due to my cholesterol situation, the doctor prescribed that I should go on statins, to keep my cholesterol level down. The result of this meant that I would have to visit the doctors every three months, for a checkup.

Jack and Harry found themselves needing a medical check-up, as part of a legal requirement, prior to going on a skiing holiday with the school. It is also necessary to have a check-up before joining a sports club. When I joined the cricket club, (yes, a cricket club in France, all will be explained in a further chapter) I had to have a clean bill of health certificate before I could play. My doctor was quite good, and filled out one for me, on one of my routine cholesterol check-ups. Not so for one of my pals, whose doctor made him do 20 press ups, and 25-star jumps, then took his blood pressure. Another friend who was a keen sportsman, had been to his doctor for certificates; to join his local cycling club and football club. It is a requirement that it is a separate one for each club. He told me that when he went to see the doctor, to ask for another sports club medical certificate, upon being told that it would be for a cricket club, the doctor laughed so much he let my mate off the €20 fee.

Back to Jack and Harrys medical, the appointment was booked, for on the way home from school. So, it was Kerry, who after first picking up Maggie from her school, made her way to the boys' school to pick them up. Maggie was too young to be left in the car, so she joined them in the waiting room. They somehow managed to squeeze in the tiny room and waited their turn. They were soon in front of the doctor, explaining the reason for their visit. The doctor, of course fully aware of the need for this medical checkup, took out his stethoscope and started to check the boys' hearts and lungs, he then moved on to check their weight and so on.

Things were going smoothly until the doctor said to the boys.
"Ok boys, I need you to strip down to your underwear, because I need to check your spine and posture."
Kerry smiled, Maggie giggled, and the boys' mouths just fell open. The doctor to help out, turned to the giggling Maggie and said,
"You can turn away young lady" which to be fair she did.

He then turned back to the boys, who like rabbits in the headlights, were frozen to the spot.
"Come, come" said the doctor "I can't carry out the necessary checks with you fully clothed."

Kerry seeing their reluctance, motivated them by saying.
"Come on do what the doctor says, you can't go skiing unless you have this medical."
They took their jumpers and shirts off but there was still a mighty reluctance about the jeans coming off.
"Come on" said Kerry "Stop messing about."
Jack gingerly slid his jeans down, to reveal a bright snazzy pair of bright orange spiderman pants. He had had these pants since he was about six years old, and today, he had somehow managed to squeeze into them. They did look a tad skimpy. Maggie, up until now, had been behaving herself, and looking the other way, but couldn't resist a glance and burst out laughing. Jack hastily explained the reason for his choice of underwear this day, was that all his other pants were in the wash. Of course!
The doctor checked Jack over and gave him a clean bill of health.

All eyes now turned on Harry.
"Come on, Harry, your turn" said Jack, hurriedly pulling his jeans up.
Harry pulled down his jeans to reveal he too had made an error of judgement in his choice of underwear that day. He was sporting a luminous green pair of pants, well what was left of them, they looked like they had suffered some sort of frenzied moth attack. Remembering Jack had already used the all the other pants in the wash excuse, Harry went for the, "it was dark when I got dressed this morning" excuse.

Maggie was in full flow with the laughter, Kerry trying to maintain composure stifled a chuckle.

Even the doctor had a smile as he checked Harry over but by the time he had finished was openly laughing.
"You English" he said, "you make me laugh; you have made my day."

Maggie doesn't come away from this type of situation squeaky clean. One day at school they had an impromptu visit from a nurse, the students formed a queue outside the medical room and were called in one at a time. When it came to Maggies turn, into the room she went. She had the usual checks – ears, eyes, height etc and then as part of the medical, Maggie was asked to strip down to her knickers. She turns to the nurse and says, "I'm sorry I can't do that."
"Why ever not" asks the nurse.
"I'm not wearing any" replies Maggie.

An equally memorable medical experience was Kerrys first trip, in France, to see a gynaecologist. She took a recommendation from a French friend who gave her the details of a place in Ploermel. This is what happened in Kerrys own words.

Upon arrival, I was asked the usual questions, about my family medical history and then, as this was my first time at this clinic, questions to my own medical history. He – the gynaecologist, yes, he, asked me, pointing to a door, to go into the next room, and remove all my clothes so I could be weighed. In the next room, I thought to myself, remove all my clothes to be weighed, I don't think so! I kept my underwear on. After all they don't weigh much. Well, when he came in to weigh me, he looked me up and down and openly sniggered. That's nice, I thought!

Things got worse when he asked me to remove my knickers and get on the "gyny" chair, which is half a bed with stirrups one end. I really wasn't happy about the request and told him I wasn't very comfortable with this. He said this is the best way for me to examine you. As there didn't seem to be an alternative, apart from grabbing my clothes and leave, which had crossed my mind. I climbed onto the chair, well as you can imagine, actually please don't, there I was, feet in the stirrups and legs akimbo with the gynaecologist at the business end.
"Cervix is looking good" he said.
If he was trying to put me at ease, it wasn't working. He then proceeds to carry out the smear test. Once he had finished and moved away from me, I shut my knees as tight as I could, wanting desperately to get off this chair. He quickly ended any hopes of that by announcing he needed to change gloves so that he could carry out a "vaginal touch." A what! Jeez when would this end. He positioned himself back between my legs and had a rummage. When he had finished and got up, I squeezed my knees back tight again. This has got to be over now, I thought hopefully. But no, removing his gloves he turns to me and asks me to take off my bra. And then while I'm totally naked, he examines my breasts. Then after what seems an eternity, it's over, I could get off the chair. I got dressed and gathered up what dignity I had left.

The cherry on the cake was that I then had to pay him! I left the clinic feeling violated, and somewhat mortified, that I had to pay for the privilege! The only thing he didn't do was knead my buttocks.

When I got home, I told Dave, thinking he would want to make a quick trip into Ploermel to have words with this geezer. Instead, his reaction was to tell me, he felt strangely aroused and took me up to the bedroom, to reclaim me!

The next time I saw my French friend who had recommended the gynaecologist. I told her what had happened, and how shocked I had been by the whole experience. She laughed and told me it was perfectly normal for France. I wasn't convinced.

The results to my tests came back and everything was all clear. There was also a note saying Mr Gyno pervert man would like to see me again in six months' time. Err no, I don't bloody think so.

A few months later, while taking French lessons, I was talking to my professor about how much I was dreading my next smear test, after my last experience. She was horrified as I recounted what had happened and told me that's not right. She recommended a female gynaecologist in another town. This time with her it was a vastly different experience, yes, I was still in the dreaded chair, but I was covered up where necessary and my dignity protected.

I never did go back to the gynaecologist at Ploermel, I live in hope that he got found out and struck off. If not, he bloody well should have.

Back to me, I had a couple of visits to hospital myself. The first one came about after I happened to mention to Dr Jean, that I had this green mouldy spot thing growing behind my left ear. This growth had affectionately been named 'green thing' by Maggie, who often asked to see it. As cute as that was, I had developed a habit of fiddling with it, and making it sore, I needed it gone.

I had had a similar spot before about ten years ago, this one was next to my right ear, but on my face, so a bit more visible. It looked like a teenage yellowhead spot; people would often stare at it and even ask me if they could squeeze it for me. But there was no popping it, it was like a hard spot and again I was prone to fiddling with it and making it sore. So, getting fed up with the soreness and the attention it was getting, I went to see my GP with a view to getting it removed. The doctor examined it and said she could remove it as part of her local surgery. An appointment was made, and I turned up at the surgery one afternoon. The doctor sat me down and started to clean around the nasty spot thing and then circled it with anaesthetic injections. The side of my face went numb, and she cut the spot off and popped it into a test tube for further examination. A couple of sterri-strips and that was that job done.

In France, however, after the doctor had examined the offending item, one quick phone call later, and an appointment was made for me, to see a consultant at the hospital in Ploermel for a few days' time. With Kerry in tow for her language skills, we found a parking space at the hospital with ease and as an added bonus, parking was free. We followed the signs to the reception and made our way in, it was more like entering a swanky hotel. It was tastefully decorated, decent artwork, nice soft furnishings, and massive plants in various locations. The receptionist was polite and friendly and directed us to our consultant's room. As we arrived at his office, he was waiting for us, we shook hands, and he invited us in. After a bit of small talk, it was down to business, and he examined the green thing. He poked and prodded it for a bit and then told us he could see no problem with having the growth removed. At the time of the appointment, there was only a week to go until Christmas. The consultant told us he couldn't fit me in this side of Christmas but asked when I was back to work in the New year. I said I'm back to work in the second week in January, checking his diary he asked if I could be on standby on the third of January. We will call you with a time at around 9AM. I agreed and with that we wished each other a Merry Christmas and a Happy New Year. And we made our way back to the car.

Christmas and the New Year festivities came and went and sure enough at 9AM on the 3rd of January the phone rang. It was the hospital receptionist telling me to be at the hospital for 1.30PM. Kerry accompanied me once again to help with any language problems, and we arrived at the hospital nice and prompt and found a parking space with ease. At reception we were guided to the minor ops section, where there was another reception. The receptionist here welcomed us both and confirmed my details. She then ushered Kerry to sit on a comfy armchair in the waiting area and asked me to follow her to a cubicle. Here, she gave me one of those flattering gowns, the type that reveal your arse, to the watching world. She then told me I would need to step into the cubicle, remove all of my clothes and put the gown on. Feeling a bit shocked by this demand and remembering how my spot had been dealt with by my doctor in England. I needed to say something.
"You do know the spot is behind my ear?" was the best I could come up with.
"Oui, oui Monsieur" she replied, "Now please go into the cubicle and put the gown on."
Was she stifling a smile as I entered the cubicle. Inside, I reluctantly did as I had been told and put the draughty

gown on. I slid back the curtains to reveal the receptionist waiting for me, she smiled and asked me to follow her. I walked along with her, down a corridor that seemed to go on for ever, all the time trying to maintain some dignity. It became a lost cause and the good people of Ploermel Hospital, staff, and fellow patients alike, were treated to the sight of my hairy, but pert butt. Eventually we arrive at some large double doors with circular glass panels. We went through the doors to reveal a proper state of the art operating theatre. There, in the centre of the room was the operating table with a large circular light suspended above it. The table was surrounded by little wheeled cabinets with all sorts of weird and wonderful implements on them. There was a bank of machines with flashing lights and dials. I was impressed but also slightly concerned that my notes had been messed up and I was the wrong room. Were they gearing up for a bit of open-heart surgery or some sort of vital organ swap. I made a mental note to confirm with the surgeon as to why I was here. On one side of the room there was a group of nurses, chatting, giggling and the occasional glance in my direction. Why so many nurses, again my thoughts wandered back to open heart surgery.

The receptionist called out to one of the nurses, beckoned her over and left. The other nurses gathered round and started talking to me in broken English. They were asking where I was from in England, where was I living now and what did I do for a job, that sort of thing. And just as I was starting to relax and enjoy the attention of these young nurses, the door burst open and in came the surgeon. I recognised him as the consultant I had met just before Christmas, so was hopeful he would know what he was here for today. He cast a disapproving eye over the group of nurses, the sort of look a teacher gives over her class as the noise level has got a bit high. The nurses gave a respectful, Bonjour and all but one of them left.

The surgeon then turned his attention to me, he welcomed me to the hospital, and we shook hands. After a brief consultation of his notes, he invited me to climb on to the table and lie on my right-hand side, so far so good. He then got a small sheet with a neat square cut out of the middle and placed it over my head with my ear, poking through the hole. I breathed a sigh of relief, he was going for the green thing, a brief irrational thought, flashed through my mind "or lop my ear off!" I quickly dismissed this and tried to relax. The massive light was turned on and the surgeon began the procedure. This began with the same cleaning and anaesthetic injections that I had experienced with my similar minor op in England. After the anaesthetic had done its job, he began to get to work with his scalpel, stopping periodically to ask if I was ok. The cutting finished, he put in five stitches and announced, he was all finished. The nasty green spotty thing was no more, I did think about asking to keep it. Perhaps a keepsake for Maggie, as she had always been fond of looking at it. As I was mulling this over, I saw the green thing being dropped into a test tube and labelled up.
"It will be sent to the laboratory for further investigation" explained the surgeon.

So, there it was, different countries, the same operation but worlds apart in procedure. The French way did seem over the top, but I guess they were leaving nothing to chance when it came to the risk of infection and the like.

A similar story is the tale of two dentists, one British and one French. A few years before we had moved to France,

I had broken a tooth eating a chocolate bar. The tooth was one of the bigger ones on the right side of my mouth, there wasn't any pain to start with. But it wasn't long before it hit with a vengeance, and how it hurt. My usual tricks of taking a mouthful of whisky and holding over the affected area or sucking a fisherman's friend on the damaged tooth, had no effect. I had to concede and go to the dentist. Lying back in his chair, he had a look and a poke around and said,
"I can fill that, it's a bit of work though and I haven't time today, you will have to come back next week."
After a painful week, I returned to the dentist to be told that my usual dentist was away on a holiday. Not to worry the temporary replacement dentist will see you. I was soon in the same dentist chair but with a different pair of eyes staring into my mouth. I heard him grunt and then announce.
"There is no way I can fill that; it will have to come out".
He gave me the necessary anaesthetic injection and sent me out into the waiting room to sit and dribble for ten minutes. I sat there wondering how they pull teeth out these days, and what new-fangled high-tech wizardry had been invented, to carry out the procedure.

My name was called out and I returned to the dentist chair. The dentist told me to relax and open my mouth, he then produced a pair of pliers. Surely not, this has got to be a joke. It wasn't and we hadn't moved on from medieval times. He gripped the offending tooth with the pliers and started to pull side to side and then up and down. It was refusing to budge.
"Bit of a stubborn bugger" he said.
He changed position which meant his knee was now resting on my chest. He carried on pulling, side to side and up and down. My head feeling the strain was moving up and down and side to side too.

"Keep your head still" he barked.
"I'm trying" I said as best as anyone could with a mouth full of pliers.

Then just when it seemed he was going to pull my head off, there was a loud crack, the dentist lurched back, and the pliers and tooth went flying in different directions. The nurse scurried over to the corner of the room, bent down, and said, "Found it!"
She bought it over to show me, the thing was massive, with a proper long root.
"That would explain the struggle" said the dentist, examining the tooth.

Moving on from that and after a couple of years of living in France, a tooth on the other side of my mouth suffered a similar fate, again while eating a chocolate bar. I will have to cut down on the chocolate, after this latest incident, or I felt I was going to have no teeth left. I suffered the pain for a bit, but as it become unbearable, the quest to find a dentist begun. We were recommended a practice in Mauron, Kerry called them up and an appointment was made. A few days later we were parking up outside the dentist surgery and remarking how modern all the medical facilities we had been to, were. It wasn't long before I was sitting in the chair, and the dentist was introducing herself. She was a young attractive woman who didn't seem much older than twenty, and she spoke good English. She was of a slight build and probably wasn't much taller than five feet, I could probably live with her climbing on me, to get a better grip with the pliers, unlike the feller in England. She examined me and said "Yes, the tooth will need to come out, but not yet, as you have an abscess. I will need to treat that first with some drugs.

She gave me a prescription which consisted of drugs for the abscess, drugs for the pain, drugs for the stomach-ache that the drugs for the pain give you. And drugs to help with the runs that all of the above give you.

All the drugs did their job and two weeks later I was back in the dentist chair. The dentist after a brief examination confirmed that the abscess was gone, and the offending tooth could come out. The gum was anaesthetised, and I was told to stay sitting in the chair and make myself comfortable. There was to be no sitting in the waiting room dribbling away in front of people here. 10 or so minutes past and she said,
"Ok that's fine, let's get that bad tooth out."
I braced myself for the struggle ahead, but she produced two strange looking hook like implements and started to work on the tooth. I couldn't feel any pain, but it felt like she was doing short jerky movements. Then suddenly there was a crack.
"Thats' got it," she said and showed me a half rotten broken tooth.
There had been no pliers in the mouth, no head thrashing from side to side or even having to fetch the tooth from the other side of the room. It was almost a pleasant experience -almost. The wound was cleaned, there was the obligatory mouthwash and that was that I was free to go.

Back to all things hospital and thankfully I was the only one to experience a French accident and emergency department. I was working in a house carrying out a large loft conversion, and access to the loft was by an open tread staircase. It was an old staircase but was made of sturdy timbers and I had wedged it against a beam. I had been working there for about 10 days and had gone up and down the stairs many, many times. But this one

afternoon, as I stepped onto the top tread, it slipped away, throwing me to one side. On the way down I bounced off the top of an open door and ended up in a heap on the floor. Jack and Kerry had joined me that day, Jack who was nearby witnessed my stuntman impression and stood there staring. As I struggled to stand up, I shouted at him "Don't just stand there, get mum, you twit" Which was a well-controlled use of language considering the pain I was in. And it was unfair to snap at Jack as he was probably in a bit of shock. He ran off and came back two minutes later with Kerry in tow. She asked me what had happened and started to check me over, her St John ambulance brigade training kicking in. My toes and fingers all wiggled OK and there appeared to be no cuts or open wounds. My left leg and arm were bruised up but by far the most painful area was around the left-hand side of my chest.
Kerry said, "It might be a good idea to get you to hospital and get you checked over."
"I'll be alright" I replied "just give me a minute to catch my breath" doing the usual macho male bit.
I sat still for about half an hour getting myself together, the pain had started to ease, and I started to feel a bit better. I stood up and started to move about, the working day had nearly finished so I made sure everything was safe and secure, tidied up and went home for a nice hot bath.

That evening, I made the mistake of watching a Peter Kay live show on TV, I had to give up after about 10 minutes as laughing was proving to be too painful. I went to bed. Now, I usually sleep on my left-hand side but that was impossible, with the pain as bad as it was. I just could not get comfortable and Kerry hearing my moans of discomfort reminded me that I really ought to go to hospital.

"I'll be fine" I hoped.
At about 4:30 in the morning still struggling to get comfortable, I sneezed. The pain suddenly doubled and half an hour later, leaving the kids unaware and still in bed, we were on our way to hospital.

We arrived at the hospital to find the car park strangely empty. We parked up and followed the signs to the 'service des urgences' - the accident and emergency department. We arrived at the main door, which happened to be a large automatic sliding door but as we stood outside, the door refused to slide. Beginning to wonder if the emergency department was closed for the night, Kerry noticed a sign that said between the hours of 11:00 PM and 6:00 PM please press this button. The button was pressed, and we waited. A couple of minutes passed and there appeared at the door, a young guy in a white jacket, wiping crumbs and other debris from around his mouth, we had obviously disturbed his breakfast. He opened the door and waved us in, and then led us up to a reception counter. Kerry explained what had happened and what the problem was.
"Ok" he said, "But first things first, I need to check your Carte Vitale."
The Carte Vitale was the health insurance card that gained you access to the French healthcare system. I gave over my card, and he inserted it into a computer and waited. After a minute or so, he turned to us, pulled out the card and gave it back and said,
"C'est Bon, now once again could you tell me what the problem is."
Like most health care staff, we had encountered he spoke an amount of English.
He took me down to a consultancy room and asked me to take my top off. He checked me over with a stethoscope and gave me a bit of a poke around the chest

area, all the time asking questions. How did it happen? When did it happen? Do I have any other pain?
"I think we will need to get the doctor to look at this" he said.
Picking up a phone he pressed a few numbers and judging by the tone and manner, the recipient on the other end had just been woken up and wasn't best pleased. The nurse guy hung up, shrugged his shoulders, and said,
"Doctors on his way"

The doctor arrived 5 minutes later, a cup of coffee in his hand and a grumpy expression on his face. He got all the details and made a quick assessment.
"You need an X-ray" he said.
He picked up the phone, punched in a few numbers and spoke to someone letting them know I was on my way. He then directed me down the corridor to the X-ray room. Reaching the room, I knocked on the door and went in, there behind a glass screen sat a nurse who looked like she too had just been woken up. Rubbing her eyes she welcomed me in and asked me to take off my shoes. She then led me onto a platform and got me to stand where an X marked the spot. She told me to stand very still and then retreated to a place of safety behind the glass screen. I watched as she pressed a sequence of buttons on a keypad and the X-ray machine sprang into life. It started to circle me, starting at my feet, going up the front of me, over my head and then down my back stopping at my feet. I had been circled. The machine shut down and the nurse asked me to return to the consultancy room.

Back at the consultancy room the doctor and the nurse were already there waiting for me, and we were soon joined by the X-ray nurse carrying a wad of large photos.

The photos were put on several screens and the three of them gathered round to have a look. There was much pointing, frowning, muttering and even some disagreement. After about 5 minutes of this it seemed they had reached an agreement. The two nurses left, and the doctor beckoned us over and pointed at one of the screens. He turned to me and said, "you have cracked your rib just here" and pointed to an area on one of the ribs on the screen.

"Oh, ok what happens now" I asked.

"Not much" he replied, "you go home, and you take it easy, and I will write you a prescription for some painkillers."

We said our goodbyes and left, it was 45 minutes since we had first arrived, and now, we were on our way home. When we got home, we found the kids were still asleep and none the wiser about our trip to hospital.

Perhaps another kind of medical story worthy of a mention concerns a friend of ours. Clive was working as a roofer; he was getting plenty of work and was doing ok. But he was doing everything under the radar, although he was providing good quality work, he hadn't taken out the necessary insurances including the accident at work insurance. Which despite being a legal requirement, most people would have thought it a complete necessity doing a job like a roofer.

One day while at work he lost his footing, slipped, and fell off the roof. He fell with a sickening thud and lay there moaning and groaning. His workmate, Tim, rushed over to him, checked he was breathing ok, and pulled out his phone and shouted,

"I'll call an ambulance."

"No" spluttered Clive "It will cost a bloody fortune, I'm not insured" and returned to his groaning.

"But you could be badly hurt," said Tim.
"I am bloody well, badly hurt" replied Clive through gritted teeth. "I've just fell off the sodding roof."
"But what are we going to do then" asked Tim.
Clive said, "Let me lie here for a bit, get me breath back and have a think."
Clive laid there wiggling his toes and then his fingers and generally checking himself over.
"I don't think I have broken anything" he said at last "but I've had an idea, fetch the blanket from the van."
Tim dutifully obliged and fetched the blanket from the van.
"Ok good, now lay it next to me," said Clive, "then help me roll on to it."
Again, Tim did his part and followed the instructions, and despite all the swearing and cursing from Clive, they managed to get him on the blanket.
"Now drag me over to the van, Tim," ordered Clive.
The manoeuvre was carried out despite the swearing and cursing, from Clive being ramped up a notch, and the odd death threat aimed at Tim for good measure. Once at the van with a good deal more of a struggle, Clive was finally in the van.
"Now get me home" said Clive "and mind the bloody bumps."
Once home the manoeuvre was reversed, and Clive was laid out next to his house and a ladder was strategically placed next to him.
"Right," said a battered and bruised Clive, "now you can call an ambulance."

The ambulance came and took him to hospital and thankfully, after a thorough check up and x-rays, it was revealed there was no serious damage. He had bad bruising and a sprained wrist and was sent home to rest for a couple of weeks.

When I saw him a few weeks later and he told me this story, I asked him if he would be taken out the insurance now.
"No" he said, "To bloody expensive, I'll take my chances."

I'll finish this chapter off with a brief story about another friend of ours. Jane was involved in a car accident which left her stunned and groggy but still sitting upright in the driver's seat. The gendarmes and the ambulance arrived, and while the gendarmes went about directing the traffic and making the area safe, the ambulance crew got to work examining Jane. Happy that she had suffered no major injuries, they eased her out of the car and onto a stretcher. They then started to remove her jumper and then removed her jeans. But when they turned their attention to removing her bra and knickers, despite her groggy state she fought back.
"What are you doing, get off me, you perverts" she screamed.
The last thing she wanted was for the small crowd of onlookers to get a free strip show. She hung onto her bra and knickers for all her worth. It must have looked quite the scene, the paramedics wrestling with a screaming, swearing, semi naked English woman. Eventually the paramedics conceded and wrapped her in a blanket, put her on the ambulance and made their way to hospital. She was sent home a few hours later with mild concussion and a story to tell.

As a conclusion, I would just like to say our experience of the French health system, the hospitals, doctors, and the rest of the staff was an extremely positive one. The hospitals and surgeries were all modern buildings and scrupulously clean and superbly functional. We know of neighbours and friends whose lives were most certainly saved by the promptness, thoroughness, and professionalism of the French healthcare staff.

Chapter Nine

This chapter deals with the pets and animals that came into our lives during our time in France. And I couldn't begin this story without mentioning the pets that joined us on our big move from England to France. All our possessions were loaded on to the removal lorry, leaving us to bring the pets over in the back of our car. Joining us in our escort estate was Dodger, our senior citizen tabby tomcat, we had had Dodger since we moved into our first house some 15 years before. He was a bit of a grumpy old git, but he was part of the family, and we felt it necessary that he joined us on our adventure. Then there was the aptly named Birdie the budgie, Birdie was looking a bit sad after pecking out all his lovely yellow feathers. This came about after his companion a blue budgie, who to avoid confusion was also called Birdie, escaped. Yellow Birdie took this quite badly and pecked all his feathers out, apart from those around his head, he couldn't quite reach them. He looked like a piece of ravioli with a yellow head. We did take him to the vets one time, and the vet after he had stopped laughing, said he's depressed, and needs cheering up. We filled his cage up with toys and mirrors, but it made little difference. As a footnote we did get him another companion some months later and gradually all his feathers grew back. And last to join us on this trip were the kids three guinea pigs. Jacks called Dexter, Harry's was called Jake and Maggie had named hers Tony, after Tony Diprose her favourite Saracens player.

Before we were to take on this trip, we had to get the necessary paperwork, and Fit to Travel documents from the vet. The guinea pigs we're all still quite young, so weren't a problem and passed their checkups fine.

However, Dodger because of his age and Birdie because of his lack of feathers, did both raise an eyebrow but were passed fit to travel. The journey was to prove to be uneventful, despite the fact, that the cat, the bird, and the guinea pigs, who in their respective carry crates, were squeezed together in the back of the car and spent the trip breathing over each other. We were stopped at customs but there were no problems, even when the customs officer asked us, if we had anything to declare. I said no, despite some very distracting but tuneful whistling coming from Birdie in the back.

In the first summer, of our new life in France, we had made friends with a young English lady named Molly, she worked occasionally at one of our neighbours' houses and we were often talking to her over the fence. One afternoon Molly knocked on our door, looking very upset. We invited her in, she sat down and explained that due to family reasons she was having to return to England. And if that wasn't bad enough, she was terribly upset about the fact she had not long took ownership of a six-month-old black labrador. She couldn't take him back with her for many reasons and was looking for someone to give him a home. Cleverly, she had asked in front of the kids and pester power now stepped in. It was agreed that she would bring him round the next day to see how he got on with the kids and of course the cat. I had a sneaky feeling that even if this dog had three legs, that the kids would ensure that next day we would be the proud owners of a black labrador.

Molly turned up the next day with her, thankfully 4-legged friend. She let him off the lead and he ran to all of us in turn, tail wagging furiously and licking us all to death. His first meeting with Dodger, was a simple and brief affair. Dodger sleeping peacefully on the chair had a big black wet nose stuck into him and Dodger responded with a couple of clawed slaps. The dog cried out and retreated, over time he was to prove, not to be the bravest of creatures. Anyway, the rules were laid down and respect was given, meaning the dog gave Dodger a wide berth from then on.

Molly bid us a tearful farewell and left us with our new pet. He came with the name Rolly, which none of us we're really keen on. The boys wanted to call him Frodo, as they were big into the Lord of the Rings at this time. We thought that would be too much of a change for Rolly to adapt to, so we settled on put in an F in front of Rolly and calling him Frolly. We did check in the French dictionary first, to make sure this didn't translate as a rude word.

Frolly settled into our home and life very nicely and gave me the excuse I needed to take on endless walks around the countryside. He was mostly a pleasure as a walking companion, although he never quite got the concept of "fetch." If you threw a ball for him, he wasn't interested. He was definitely of the school of thought "well you threw it, you get it." Instead, he was much happier, without any warning, running off and sprinting in ever increasing circles around a field, while I watched on bemused. He also had a thing for aircraft, we didn't get that many fly over us. The occasional light aeroplane and some days the military practising in their jets and helicopters. If a plane did have the audacity to fly over the garden, Frolly would run out barking, in its direction while all the time standing on his hind legs. One regular morning dog walk, Frolly was off the lead when a large military transport plane flew by at low level – hedge hopping I believe they call it. The ramp at the back of the aircraft was down, it was that close and low, that I could make out the aircrew standing at the back. Frolly taking exception to this intruder gave a loud bark and gave chase. I could quite clearly see the crew pointing and laughing at this black labradors valiant attempt to catch them and see them off. Despite all my shouting for him to come back, he kept going until he was a small black dot in the distance. I stared after him shaking my head. He eventually stopped when he came up against a hedgerow, he turned round and started to stroll back. As the aeroplane disappeared into the distance, I sat down on a grassy bank and waited for the hero to return.

One time when walking through the Lanouee Forest, a massive forest full of deer, boar and in the hunting season - the worst animal of all; the hunters! We were walking along a path when suddenly just ahead of us there appeared a massive stag. It was a magnificent beast with an impressive set of antlers, it stopped and eyed us cautiously. This didn't impress Frolly, who gave one of his best hunting howls and started running towards the stag. Equally unimpressed was the stag who stood his ground. Frolly realising the stag, had no intention of running off, skidded to a halt. Dog and stag eyeballed each other for a bit, until Frolly assessing the situation turned round and jogged back to us. The stag stared after us with what appeared to be a look of contempt, he snorted and disappeared into the undergrowth.

Overtime Folly's hunting prowess developed; we would be out walking when suddenly his nose would hit the ground. He would run around frantically in tight circles, his nose still centimetres from the ground, sniffing feverishly. Then his head would lift up, he would let out a massive howl, that wouldn't have been out of place in the Hounds of the Baskerville. Howling over, he would then run off at full speed, barking as he went. The first

time he did this, I was walking alone, and I stood staring in amazement at what was happening in front of me. I tried to give chase, shouting his name as I went but all I could hear was his barks disappearing into the distance. I searched for him for over an hour and then gave up and went home. Arriving home I went into the kitchen where Kerry was, and said "well that's great, I've lost the dog."
"No, you haven't," replied Kerry, "he's in the lounge behind the settee."
I peered over the back of the settee and there was this black lump puffing and panting for all his worth. He had made his own way home.

The boys, had great delight in telling me a tale of when the pair of them, took Frolly out for a walk. One of them who shall remain nameless – Jack, did a little blow off but unfortunately had a slight follow through. Apparently, it was one of them, hard little marble type turds. With a slight adjustment of underwear and a shake of the leg, the offending item rolled down Jacks trouser leg and onto the ground, upon which, Frolly promptly ate it, much to the delight and hysterical laughter of the boys. Dirty dog.

On a sadder note, in the first autumn of living in France, we lost Dodger who passed away in his sleep. He was buried in the garden under a large quartz rock, which is still there to protect his memory.

After Christmas we acquired some chickens, there was Rocky the cockerel and his little harem of 5 hens. Rocky was your typical proud and strutting cockerel. He was ugly enough to be cute as he had no feathers around his neck, but we were told this was normal for this breed of cockerel. He was quite young when we got him and hadn't reached the cockle doodle doo stage yet. After a few weeks, he began to try and had managed several half assed attempts, until one morning he nailed it. We were lying in bed when we heard a clearly distinct cockle doodle doo. We were like proud parents whose child had just said his first word. After his first successful attempt was completed, he wouldn't shut up, pleased with himself he spent the rest of the day cockle doodle doing.

Rocky seemed to grow in stature with his newfound maturity and took firm control of his harem. In the morning, he was always first out of the hen house when it was opened up. Once out he would quickly hide behind the door and lie in wait for the first hen to come out. Once the first hen had stepped out, he would leap on them and much to their annoyance, as the muttering would suggest, he would have his wicked way with them. After a while, the hens became wise to this and would hold back from coming out, hoping Rocky would get bored and wander off for something to eat. Despite this his girls did respect his leadership. One evening, at lockup time at the hen house, Rocky was nowhere to be seen. A comprehensive search of the garden and surrounding area revealed nothing, not even a pile of feathers that would suggest a struggle with a predator. The hens didn't settle that night, and in the morning, there wasn't any eggs for us to collect. The hens weren't happy at all, they were off their food and spent most of their day in a huddle, muttering. As the day progressed from afternoon into the evening and just as we were thinking that's the last, we'll ever see of Rocky. We heard the sound of the hens clucking excitedly and then a distinct cockle doodle doo, it was Rocky, he was back. And peace and harmony was restored to the hen house.

That first spring in Brittany and a trip to the local market, echoed to the sound of poultry – cockerels, hens, chicks, and ducklings. The kids rather taken with the ducklings decided between them that they would rather like one each for Easter presents. We couldn't see the harm and made the purchase. All was good while they were small, cuddly, yellow, and cute. They would sit on the kids laps while they watched telly, follow them around the garden and play with them in the paddling pool. After a few weeks it was like they had become grown up adult ducks, overnight. Gone were the cute yellow balls of fluff and instead we had these big lairy noisy individuals. They became very messy, the garden mostly awash with duck shite. Just as well they were banned from the house by now. But worst of all they started to upset the chickens, they ate all the food and generally made nuisances of themselves, resulting in the hens stopping laying. The decision was made, they had to go.

Someone did suggest we kill them and eat them but that didn't prove to be popular with the rest of the family. A solution presented itself when a friend of a friend, said she was after some ducks for her pond and her cat had just had kittens. How about an exchange? So that was how the next pet to join the family came to be. We swapped our thug ducks for a rather handsome and cute little kitten, that we named Monty. I am not the greatest of cat fans, I would rather see wild birds in the garden than a cat. But Monty soon endeared himself to me. He was a hairy tabby and as he grew older, someone told us, he looked like a Maine Coon breed; he certainly was a handsome fella. He was also to prove; he had a great personality and character but was soon using up some of his nine lives. Two incidents spring to mind, once I was walking through the lounge and saw Monty hanging by his paws from the top of the stairs. At the time the staircase was opened tread. Before I could get to him, he lost his grip and fell but landed straight in Maggies dolls pram, where the bedding cushioned his fall. Although this time the pram had saved him from harm, he would soon come to despise this said pram. Maggie would enjoy dressing Monty up in dolls clothes. She particularly liked dressing him up in a baby grow and taking him out in the pram for a walk around the hamlet. Monty despite his struggling could not move because of the restrictions put on him by wearing the baby grow. One time, Maggie was approached by an elderly lady who asked to see her baby, she was rather taken aback, when she peeped in the pram to see a rather disgruntled cat staring back at her.

Back to using up his nine lives, another time Maggie ran into the house shouting.
"Help! Come quick, Monty is stuck up a tree and cannot get down."
We all rushed out into the garden and there sure enough was this little kitten hanging on to the last lone branch at the top of a tree. I went off to get a ladder while Kerry went in the house to get a blanket. Returning, I placed the ladder against the tree, and Kerry, Jack, Harry, and Maggie stood holding the blanket at each corner underneath Monty's position in case he should fall. Thankfully, this wasn't necessary, as I climbed up the ladder and edged closer to him, I stretched out my hand and he gratefully accepted my rescue attempt and came to me without much of a fuss.

Even though he was a tiny little thing as a kitten, he used to lie in wait under hedges and bushes and leap out with a flying star jump at any unsuspecting passerby. He got on well with Frolly, and apart from competition for the best place in front of the fire there was hardly ever a problem between them. He grew into a big handsome fluff ball of a cat. He was smart and clever, although running out and laying on his back when we reversed up the drive was never one of his best ideas. And always ended up with one of the kids jumping out of the car to pick him up.

If we fast forward to a few years' time when we had made the decision to move back to England, Monty was to prove just how clever and smart he really was. A few months before the date of our return to England we had the problem of what to do with our pets. Homes were found for the smaller creatures, the budgies, hamsters etc, our big concerns were Frolly and Monty. They were both used to the countryside with its wide-open spaces and very little traffic. It was agreed there was no way we were leaving Frolly behind, we felt he could be taught and could adapt to his new surroundings. He would have to be kept on his lead a lot more and would have to learn how to socialise with other dogs. With Monty it was a different story, as much as he was a loved member of the family, we all felt that moving back to England would be hard on him. He was used to roaming far and wide, he was not road savvy and the increased traffic in England would be a problem. We did not want to take him back and he ends his life run over and lying in the gutter. He would never have taken to being a house cat either, so when some friends offered to take him on, we all agreed that this was for the best.

A month before we were due to leave, we took the forty-five-minute drive over to our friends house, so that Monty could start his life in a new home. We thought this would be the right thing to do, so if there were any problems we were still around to help. Our friends had cleared a small room for Monty so he could stay shut in for the time being, until he acclimatised to his new surroundings. Our friends already had a cat, and it was thought better to keep them away from each other for the time being. There were lumps in our throats as we said our goodbyes and understandably some tears from Maggie.

A few days passed when we had the phone call we were dreading, Monty had escaped and was nowhere to be seen. We drove over to our friends' house and spent the afternoon scouring the surrounding countryside. We took Frolly with us in the hope he could help and perhaps sniff him out, or even that Monty would hear him and recognise a friendly voice. After many hours we had to admit defeat and gave up. We came back the next day to resume our search but again it proved fruitless. Our friend said they would leave food out and a window open in case he came back.

Three weeks later we moved back to England, Monty's disappearance had left a bad taste in our mouth. We had managed to sort out all the other pets but had no idea as to Monty's' fate. We had moved back to England in the first week of September and fell into the grind of trying to find work and the kids starting their new schools and college.

At the end of September, I had a phone call from our neighbour in France, which went something like this,
"Morning Dave, just to let you know, when I got up this morning and opened the front door, there was your cat, Monty, on the doorstep."
When I had picked up my jaw from the floor, I asked how he was.
"He looks fine" came the answer, "he has lost a bit of weight, but he is more or less the same old Monty.

The neighbour agreed to look after him until the next time we were down.
Hanging up the phone I could not believe it. I even got the map out and tried to work out the distance Monty would have travelled. It looked like it was about thirty miles, crossing rivers, one canal, an autoroute and several other roads. This journey had taken him eight weeks - such a clever Kitty.

Of course, Maggie was over the moon when I told her, and we hastily booked a trip down to France for the next half term. We also agreed he had deserved the right to stay with us, he would just have to be a house cat.

A friend still living in France, having heard of Monty's adventure contacted me by e-mail, saying that he had friends, who lived a couple of miles down the road from Treblou. Their cat had recently passed away, and they were looking at taking another one on. I told him I was not sure what the plan was at the moment, Maggie wanted to bring him home, but all the reasons that we had left him in France, were still there.

Before long, half term arrived, and Maggie and I found ourselves reversing up our drive and there was Monty. He ran out and lay on his back on the drive, like we had not been away. Maggie Jumped out the car and with tears in her eyes gave him a big hug. He looked in good condition, there were no signs of wear and tear from his epic adventure.

The next day we went to the local vets to find out what paperwork we would need to put in place to take Monty back to the UK. While we were trying to explain ourselves to the receptionist as to what we needed, we were approached by a couple, who had been standing behind us in the queue. They said they were sorry to interrupt but were we the owners of Monty the cat, that we've heard so much about. It turns out that they were the couple that my friend had emailed me about, that had lost their cat and were after taking on a new one. What are the chances of them being in the vets, the same time as we were! We got chatting and they told us all about their cat that they had lost, their home and their dog. It seems the dog was similar to Frolly in looks and didn't have a problem with cats. They seemed like a nice couple, and we agreed to go around their house and take Monty with us to meet them. The house and the lovely big garden ticked all the boxes. And the lumbering old Labrador would make Monty feel right at home. This seemed like an opportunity for Monty, to keep him in the life that he was used to. They were only 5 minutes down the road from Treblou, so should he get the homing instinct again he wouldn't have far to go. I spoke to Maggie, and she reluctantly agreed it was in Monty's best interests to leave him there.

So that's what happened, we left Monty for a second time, happy that he still had his open spaces and freedom to enjoy. We checked up on him from time to time, we were over the moon, to hear that this time he had settled in fine.

Returning to 2002, the next animals to join our growing menagerie were rabbits. A neighbour popped round one evening and told us she was having to get rid of her rabbits. They had taken the blame for aggravating her asthma, so they had to go. She said they lived in her Conservatory and even used a litter tray, well most of the time. They were a cute pair of rabbits who wouldn't have looked out of place in a Disney movie. They were predominantly white with small black patches and floppy ears. They were named Dylan of course and Dylan 2. We gave them a go at being house bunnies but using the litter tray most of the time, in reality was using the litter tray not really at all. The next day I built them a hutch and they were consigned to the garden. A friend visiting one day claim to be knowledgeable about sexing rabbits. Upon inspection it was discovered that Dylan was a male and Dylan 2 a female, her name was swiftly changed to Lilo and another hutch built, two rabbits was enough for now.

In the summer we allowed the rabbits out for a run in the garden but even then, they were kept separated. One was kept in a run while the other had the free run of the garden. One day the urge must have got too much for Dylan and using all his strength had leapt the fence to join up with Lilo. He then proceeded to do what rabbits generally do but being a bit of a novice, he was bouncing about on Lilo's head. Maggie witnessing the spectacle and seeing his plight, stepped into the run, and put him in the right place. She told us all about it over dinner that evening.

While I was feeding the rabbits a few weeks later, I noticed that Lilo had built a nest and on closer inspection, revealed seven little bunnies. Great! We are going to need more hutches and before long, Bunny Towers was conceived and constructed.

Another sunny Saturday morning and another visit to our favourite market in Josselin, to buy fresh fruit and veg and to have breakfast, of a 'galette saucisse.' This is a typical French street food item consisting of a hot sausage wrapped in a buckwheat crepe. Wandering down one of the aisles, we heard the sound of clucking, which meant we were getting close to the poultry man's stall.

Looking over to his stall, it was pointed out that he had some goslings for sale. Jack edged forward, had a brief word with the market trader, he produced a few euros and suddenly, was the proud owner of two goslings. They were small and cute at this stage, so it didn't seem too much of a problem. Sadly, one of them died after a couple of weeks but the other one went from strength to strength and grew big and strong. But with that strength came aggression, we think it possibly started when Harry came home with a pal from school. Harry was introducing him to our menagerie when the goose, who Jack had named Britney, went for Harrys pal. We were to find out later, that Harrys school friend, lived on a chicken farm. The farm wasn't for the chickens' eggs, it was for their meat, so whether he had the smell of death on him, we will never know. But whatever it was, it certainly had upset Britney, who was now very protective off her territory and would only allow Jack and myself up the back garden. Kerry had even to be protected when she went up the garden to hang the washing out. Harry and Maggie declared the back garden a no-go zone. Meanwhile Jack could wander up the garden, sit down and Britney would waddle over, sit between his legs facing him and rest her head on his shoulder. They would sit there for ages having this cuddle. If Jack wasn't about, even the chickens became a target, Britney would jump on the unsuspecting bird, pin it down and pull out a beak full of feathers.

However, Britney's' life was to come to a premature end when she went lame, it looked like she had broken one of her legs. I had learnt that with the keeping of livestock comes the unpleasant reality of dealing with sick and injured birds that have to be humanely dealt with. I had already had to deal with one sick and dying hen. I owned a .22 rifle, a powerful gun that I had bought, for dealing with situations such as this. I took the poor unfortunate bird out of the garden and into the back field with the intention of shooting it. I didn't fancy the traditional method of wringing its neck, I'm not very good at that kind of thing, and killing things is not something I enjoy. I am definitely not one of life's hunters, I have always been a live and let live kind of person. And anyway, I'd heard tales of people wringing a chicken's neck and the head coming off!

I placed the hen on the ground, backed away, loaded the rifle, took aim, and fired. There was a puff of feathers, and the dirt kicked up behind her, the bullet had gone right through. It hadn't been enough to kill the bird, in fact, she tilted her head towards me and looked at me as if to say "Oi, what did you do that for?" I couldn't believe it, I aimed and fired again. There was the same puff of feathers and the kick up of dirt but as before, she just sat there but looking even more annoyed now. An unpleasant thing to do was becoming even more unpleasant. I fired again and this time it did the job. Getting back to Britney's plight there was no way I was going to attempt to shoot her after the hen fiasco. Something needed to be done though, she looked a pitiful sight just sitting in the corner of the hen house, in her own mess. I read up on the most humane way to kill a goose. The most popular method seemed to be to use two broom handles, lay one on the floor, place the gooseneck on the handle and the other one across the neck. And then using your feet to stand on the handles, twist the bird and thus breaking its neck – delightful. Oh well, it had to be done. I set it up, and after half an hour of trying, there was distressed honking, and feathers, and shit flying everywhere. I decided this was neither quick, nor humane, so I took the decision to just stand on the

handles and choke her, one of the most unpleasant things I've ever had to do.
But from sadness, peace and tranquillity returned to the garden. Chickens and humans could wander around the garden in safety once more.

In the house, some unwanted guests were discovered, while investigating a strong mousy smell, our noses led us to Maggies' room and ultimately her litter bin. Lifting the lid revealed two mice, snuggled up in a nest made from scrap paper. When Maggie came home from school, we quizzed her on her two guests.
"Oh, Mickey and Minnie" she said, "They have been there about a fortnight, I have been feeding them on scraps from the table and fruit."
We told her they had to go; they stank! A compromise was reached, in that we would release Mickey and Minnie up the woods and there would be no more guests in her bedroom, if we got her a hamster.

It wasn't long before we were on our way to the town of Vannes, to visit the big pet shop that we knew. While walking across the car park, our attention was drawn to a harassed mother, walking to her car accompanied by two very animated children, both boys, one being around eight, the other about 10 years old. The older boy was carrying one small cardboard box, the nature of the box suggested that there was a small animal inside it. The mum opened the boot and turned her attention to the bags of shopping. Meanwhile the younger boy put his hand in the box and pulled out a small green parrot, he threw it into the boot of the car and the older boy slammed the boot lid shut. But it was too late, the parrot flew through the gap and took to the air, it circled the car park once and then disappeared over the building. The boys stared at each other while their harassed mother had some sort of meltdown.

After Maggie had got her hamster home and settled into her bedroom, thankfully in a cage and not in her bin. Harry decided for his birthday he would quite like a pet for his bedroom and settled on having a rat. On his birthday he chose a large black and white fancy rat that he named Fleur. The following story about Fleur was published in an expats magazine, after I had sent it in. This is how it appeared:

A Rats Tale by Dave Brewer
Its Harrys 13th birthday and he has decided he would like his own pet to take care of and to look after - it is a rat. So, we take a trip to Vannes, to visit a big pet shop that we know. Inside the shop and after much deliberation, he chooses a black and white female rat, that he names Fleur. The new arrival settles into her new home and shiny cage in Harry's bedroom. Things are going just fine until on the sixth day there is an excited shriek from Harry's bedroom.
"Fleurs had babies" he shouted.
And so, she had, twelve of them.
"Can I keep them" asked Harry.
"No way!" came the reply from Kerry, who hurries off to phone the pet shop. After a bit of giggling from the lady at the pet shop she says yes, we will take the babies, after all, you have only paid for one! Who said the French don't have a sense of humour. She says to bring them in when they are 4 weeks old and can safely leave their mother. The days pass and Fleur proves to be a good mother, mum and baby are doing fine. A couple of days before the babies are due to be taken back to the pet shop, Harry announces that one of the babies has escaped! He was playing with them on his bed and one

of them had slipped away, without him noticing. Great, so now we have a rat loose in the house. In the morning there is more bad news from Harry's bedroom, he had left the door open in the roof of the cage in case the baby came back; and now Fleur has escaped! After much investigation, listening and searching, we realise that Fleur and the baby have joined up, and without taking down walls, or doing any other damage, we have worked out the best place to recapture them. We take it in turns, screwed up into a little ball behind the water heater, armed with a small net, but with no success. The day to take the remaining babies to the pet shop arrives, so we leave for Vannes with eleven babies and a mummy and baby rat still loose in our house. The man in the pet shop is tickled by our story and asks why we are not keeping any of the babies, in case, we can't capture the two runaways. We decline and leave the shop with his last words still in our heads.
"Be careful that the baby that escaped isn't a boy, otherwise it could mean more babies."
Great, a rat infestation, just great.
Harry tries to reassure us, by telling us he was sure that the baby escapee was a girl. How would he even know that?

While in Vannes, we did purchase a rat sized humane trap. Later that day the trap was placed behind the water heater with a bait of chocolate. After two days of chocolate, we still have no rats, so we changed the bait to cheese, still no success. On the fifth day we changed the bait to a piece of watermelon, and it was an instant success, in no time we had captured Fleur. Who was not too pleased to be back in her cage. Later that evening we heard the trap door slams shut, and we had the baby. At last, no more rats running loose in the house and Monty was taken off his house ban.

In the morning Harry cheers us up by telling us that in the night Fleur had somehow bent the bars of the cage allowing the baby to escape again. However, it was a short-lived spell of freedom, as the baby fell victim to the watermelon in the trap once more. The smiles were to turn to frowns, when it was discovered that the baby was a boy. After this revelation, the two rats were separated, but they had spent many days together and who knows what went on behind the water heater. It's getting to that time again when we hear the shriek from Harry's room, meaning, here we go again….

Another cage was acquired, and the baby became Jacks bedroom pet, he called it Indie.

The rats weren't the only escape artists, that Harry kept in his bedroom. While out exploring one day, he found a lizard. He got himself a small fish tank, put a few rocks and some foliage in it, and as he put the lizard in it said, "welcome to your new home." The lizard obviously didn't feel welcome, and soon escaped. Harry told us, he thought it was living in the wall. It had been living somewhere, because three weeks later, it turned up in Jacks bedroom, where it was captured. Harry was pleased, but we said "perhaps, it should be returned to the wild." After some thought, Harry agreed and took the lizard back to where he had found it and let it go.

After a couple of years of being in France, Sonny came into our lives. Sonny was a golden Labrador, he was of a slight build, not as stocky as Frolly, and had a dent in his head where he was attacked by another dog when he was a puppy. It had affected him physically and mentally if some of the things he got up to were anything to go by. Sonny belonged to Kerrys brother, Martin, but they were moving into rented accommodation for a spell and couldn't take Sonny with them. Frolly and Sonny had met before and had got on fine, so taking him on wasn't considered an issue. Sonny was a lovely natured dog, although he did have this annoying habit of randomly letting out a loud bark for no apparent reason, and when you were least expecting it. He was also at his happiest when he had something in his mouth, usually a sock but it could be shoes, slippers, or anything really. You left these types of things laying around at your peril. It wasn't unusual to go up the garden or even up the woods, or around the lane and find a long-lost slipper that Sonny had been carrying around, until something else had taken his fancy. Large branches were also of interest, he would often come charging towards us with half a tree in his mouth, scattering everyone in his wake. One of the first times we took him out, along with Frolly, of course, was in the nearby massive Lanouee Forest. We had been walking sometime, when all of a sudden, Sonny ran off. Frolly joined him for a short distance but answering our shouts to come back, surprised us all, by actually doing just that. Sonny, meanwhile, kept going and was soon out of sight. Jack and Harry sprinted after him, shouting his name as they went but with no luck. They came back and told us, "There's no sign of him, he's gone." What were we to do, as I have mentioned, this forest, is enormous. Great, I thought, we've had Sonny five minutes, and I've got to ring Martin up tonight and tell him I have lost his dog. We hatched a plan to split up and meet up back at the car, in an hour. The forest is laid out in grids, with tracks dividing these grids, so forestry works can be carried out. I went off with Maggie, and Kerry set off in the other direction with the boys and Frolly. We covered as much distance as we could, shouting out for Sonny as we went. The hour up, we found our way back to the car, where we were the first to arrive. Ten minutes later, around the corner came

Kerry, the boys, Frolly and happily, they had Sonny too. Kerry explained that they had found him with another family. He had latched onto them, enjoying their company and their picnic. Stupid Sonny, but at least we had him back. Another Sonny moment was when we were out on a family stroll, one chilly autumn afternoon. He took it on himself to leap into a pond, after a brief swim, he emerged and shook himself off. We carried on walking but, five minutes later, it was noticed that he was shivering really bad. We were still some way from the car, so Maggie had to give up her anorak. We managed to squeeze it on him, he soon stopped shivering, and he looked very fetching in his pink coat. He even got some compliments from fellow dog walkers.

Harry took both dogs out one afternoon, armed with a pocket full of those tiny bangers, that are readily available and popular with children in France. He arrived at the woods, lit a banger up and threw it. Now Sonny unlike Frolly, was familiar with and would embrace the game of fetch. Seeing Harry throw the banger he took off after it. He would have grabbed hold of it, had Harrys despairing dive not caught Sonny's tail and stopped him in his tracks. The banger went off, and the loud bang was amplified by the still and quiet of the woods. Frolly ran off and was next found in the lounge hiding behind the settee, while Sonny stood there tail wagging, looking at Harry as if to say do it again.

The two years that we had Sonny were good. The dogs were great company for each other, and they shared a bed in the kitchen. At times, Frolly would prefer it, if their bed was in the lounge and would drag it from the kitchen, with Sonny asleep on it, not moving, as he was bumped down the step into the lounge. There was an armchair in the corner of the lounge, that was put there especially for the dogs to use. Obviously, they would both want to lie on it at the same time, which often ended up in a battle for supremacy, a brief wrestling match, with them taking turns to lay on top of one another.

On our many dog walking expeditions, despite being a remote area we would sometimes bump into people. There was this one lady, probably in her sixties, who we used to see being dragged around the countryside by her collie type dog. She used to really struggle to keep him in check, he was a lot stronger than she was. We did use to stop and talk to her and found out that she lived in a nearby hamlet, we also found out that the dog's name was Loopy, which seemed appropriate, although not sure how it translated. After many months of bumping into her and exchanging small talk, one day she told us she was going away for a few days and couldn't find anyone to look after Loopy. She said she had noticed how well he got on with Frolly and Sonny, so would we mind looking after her dog. We expressed uncertainty because of Monty and the chickens but agreed on a trial visit one morning. A couple of days later and Loopy is dropped off and Madame departs. The first thing that Loopy does, is to try and savage Monty. Loopy chases Monty around the house scattering everything in his path, but fortunately Monty manages to escape by jumping out of a window and seeking safety on the shed roof. Not a good start and Loopy is banished to the front garden.

Things seem to calm down and we go about our daily chores, this doesn't last too long as we hear more bedlam coming from outside. We rush out to see that Loopy has jumped the four-foot fence and has a neighbours white poodle pinned to the ground. There is white fur flying everywhere, I grab a broom and try to prize Loopy off the poodle. This doesn't work so I give Loopy a couple of well-aimed thwacks with the broom handle. This does the trick; Loopy let's go of the poodle and the poodle runs home looking like a trip to the parlour is in order. There is a lot of white fur, but it doesn't look like there is any evidence of blood. Loopy spends the rest of the morning chained up.

Madame comes back at lunchtime, seeing Loopy chained up she hesitantly asks how it went. We explained what happened and she was a bit taken aback and offered us her sincere apologies for Monty, the furniture, and the neighbours poodle.

The next day she appeared at our door clutching an oven ready chicken, it was a gift to apologise for our inconveniences. It was a bit of an odd gift, but we received it gratefully. She also went down the lane to see the poodle's owner to apologise, and we learned later that she had also bought them an oven ready chicken. Very practical these Breton folk.

Not really a pet story but worthy of entering in this section as it's about an animal. Pottering about in the front garden one Monday, I heard our neighbour, Eve shout out, "Hello Frolly, what are you doing here."

That's strange I thought, as Frolly was lying about two metres away from me.

Eves' shouts turn to shrieks, and I hurry out of the gate to investigate. And trotting up the lane, comes a massive, grizzled old, snaggly toothed boar. The creature was huge and carried the scars of a tough life. I backed off into the garden and shut the gate. The boar went into Renes' garden, did a quick lap, and disappeared up the lane. Moments later, Renes' front door opened and there he stood in his Y-fronts, scratching himself and wondering what it was that had just been in his garden.

Eve told me later that she had been hanging out her washing, when a dark creature had brushed by her, she first thought it was Frolly, but when she looked down, she saw this massive boar tramping through her daffodils.

The boar was the talk of the hamlet for a couple of days. There had been many sightings and even a couple of attempts to catch it. Including one by a feller who tried to knock it down in his car but ended up in a ditch while the boar made his escape.

Front views of the house

A drawing of the house by Jack aged 13

Maggie in the kitchen in the early days...

How the kitchen looks now.

Kerry working hard and sporting our company logo shirt!

Posing for our first Christmas in France

The BBC 'Inside Out' crew and us

Me wrapped up in red tape for the BBC!

Maggie in the lounge in the early days...

...and as it looks now

View of the lake...

...and including the footbridge.

View of the lake looking towards the road...

...and with prehistoric stones in the foreground.

Frolly and Sonny...

Harry and Maggie with Frolly.

Sharing the warmth of the fire...

...and Frolly living the dream!

Frolly and Sonny in their favourite chair...

...and in a stand-off
over 'THEIR' chair!

Surprise, surprise baby bunnies!

Rocky the cockerel and his girls.

The ducklings enjoying the paddling pool...

...Maggie and her famous duck balancing act!!

Maggie and her duck - not so cute
anymore...that's the duck not Maggie!

Harry and his pet rat - Fleur...

Jack enjoying a cuddle with his goose - Britney!

First day owning Monty - he was such a cute kitty...

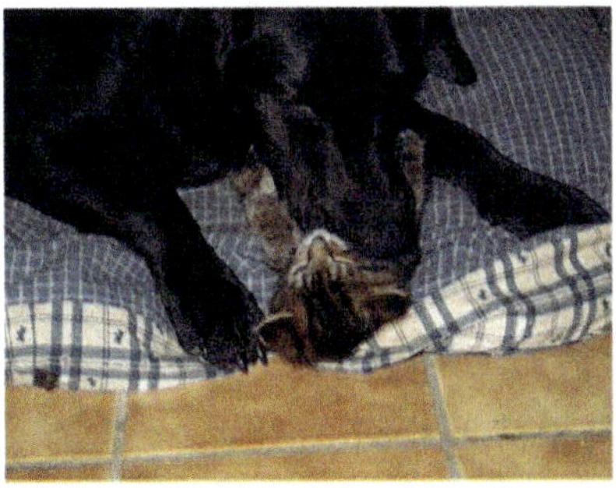

Frolly welcomes Monty...

...Monty all grown up!

Cricket in Brittany with Jack, Harry and me

Me and the boys before *that* football match; it must be before as there are hints of a smile and we're not all sweaty

Chapter Ten

This chapter deals with some of our many sporting activities we got up to. Some of them were garden based like table tennis, basketball, archery, and darts with a blowpipe, etc. And then there was all the non-garden-based sports, so I'll start with fishing.

I have been a keen angler, starting from a young age. I had got the kids into fishing, before we moved to France, and they seemed to enjoy it too. Many a lovely day was spent fishing on the River Beult, in the heart of the Kent countryside. It was a lovely spot, with an abundance of fish, and great for pike; or as Harry told everyone after a memorable days fishing, "Dad caught a prick today."

Living in Treblou we were lucky to have a pond, two minutes' walk down the lane from us. I had made a deal with the owner, that if we maintained it, that is, kept the grass and weeds strimmed and any tree branches cut back, we could fish it. We had many a happy session down there, and being so close to home it wasn't unusual for Monty to wander down and join us. It was also convenient for ringing up home and getting Kerry to pop down with a couple of cold beers if I got thirsty.

On one of my dad's summer visits, we were talking about fishing, and he said the only time he had been, was when he took me on my first fishing trip, when I was about nine. An Uncle had given me a rod, reel, and some basic tackle. So naturally I had been pestering Dad to take me out. Eventually he conceded and joined the fishing club at work, and took me to Rose Court Lake, out on the Isle of Grain. As we were setting up, I began to realise, that dad, knew about as much as me, as to the art of angling; nothing! We didn't know the knot for tying the hook, how to set the float and weights up, or even how

to cast. Every attempt at a cast, ended up in a massive birds' nest tangle, at the end of the rod. After an hour of frustration, a bit of swearing and yet another tangle to deal with, Dad finally broke, and shouted, "I've had just about enough of this."
Now, Dad used to smoke in them days and threw his cigarette down in disgust, which amazingly ended up in his boot. It was burning his ankle, and the swearing increased as he leapt around trying to take his boot off.

This commotion had attracted the attention of a nearby angler who came along to see what the fuss was about. He recognised dad from work, and when he had stopped laughing, he set about helping us and gave me my first lesson in fishing. He showed me how to set up a basic float rig, how to tie a hook and how to cast – stupid reel with its stupid bail arm, we didn't know you had to flip it to one side to be able to cast and then flip it back once the cast was made. Despite the pain of this first trip, I became a keen angler, Dad on the other hand, hasn't been seen by the lake or riverside ever since.

So back to that sunny summers' afternoon in Treblou and our discussion about fishing. It seemed the perfect time to take Dad on his second fishing trip. I gathered some rods and tackle together and opened a tin of sweetcorn, to use as bait. Off we went, and on the way down, Dad turned to me and in a concerned voice said, "Oi, hold on a minute, there aren't any bloody snakes down here, are there?"
"Well, I have never seen one" I replied, "And I have done lots of work here, mowing, strimming, clearing, as well as lots of fishing, and I have never seen one."
Dad has got a fear of snakes practically a phobia, but he seemed happy with my reasoning.

Once by the pond, I found him a nice spot, set up his rod and did his first cast for him. The float settled nicely on the calm water, the orange tip of the float nicely visible in the afternoon sunshine.
"Right, that's you all sorted" I said, "All you have to do now is watch your float."
I moved a few metres along the bank and began to set up. I had hardly got my rod out of the bag, when I heard, "What does it mean when the float disappears," shouted dad.
"Quick, grab your rod, you've got one" I replied.
But before anything else could happen, the rod leapt off the rod rests and landed with a splash in the water. I ran over to him with the landing net, and swung it into the water just managing to trap the end of the rod and reel and pulled it in. I started to reel the line in, but there was no resistance, the fish had got away. I put some fresh bait on the hook, and cast out again, giving nice and clear instructions as to what to do in the event of a bite.

Returning to my own gear, I carried on setting up. I was just about at the baiting the hook stage, when another shout rang out,
"Oi! What the bloody hell is that then," cried dad.
I looked out across the pond, and there gliding across the smooth surface was a large grass snake, probably about a metre long. I couldn't believe it.

Well, that was the end of that fishing trip, and a few moments later, we were walking back up the lane to home. I hadn't even managed to bait my hook. After a few beers and over dinner, the snake according to dad that is, was getting longer and longer and I'm sure by the end of the evening was nearer the four-metre mark.

When we were packing for our big move to France, I had included my large cricket bag complete with bat, pads, whites, etc. Kerry had raised an eyebrow, and asked,
"Why on earth are you taking that, I don't think you'll be playing much cricket where we are going."
Not wishing to give my cricket stuff up just yet, I remained hopeful as it was the one sport I was half decent at.
"Well, you never know" was my defence.

And how prophetic that turned out to be. After a couple or so years of being in France, I was looking on one of the ex-pat websites, when I noticed a message from someone about starting a cricket club up. They were after feedback to see if there was any interest in starting such a venture. My interest was pricked, so I replied. I found out it was to be based in Josselin, about fifteen minutes' drive away, so not too bad, and I was invited to the next meeting. The meeting was held in a house on the edge of Josselin, it was relatively easy to find, because of the Brit motors parked outside it. I knocked on the door and was greeted by someone who looked like W.G Grace, a nice touch I thought. With his long beard moving in the evening draught, he invited me in. I entered the lounge, and a beer was placed in my hand, and I was offered a seat. I introduced myself, shook everyone's hand and sat down. I looked around at the other prospective cricketers, thankfully I wasn't the oldest, but I wasn't the youngest either. That accolade went to the four French lads who were probably in their late twenties and didn't speak a word of English. Had they even heard of cricket? The other six, were about my age or older. It turned out to be an enjoyable evening, lots of ideas were banded about, and lots of cricket talk and banter.

As I drove home, I mulled over the prospects of this cricket team. At this moment, we didn't have enough players, the French lads had driven to us from Gourin, a drive of about an hour and a half. And were keen, in time, to set up a team local to them. So, we couldn't rely on them, that took us down to six players. We had no kit or pitch to play on. The nearest opposition team was near Mont St Michel, at a campsite at Des Ormes, a ninety-minute drive away. And the nearest other team was at Saumur, in the Loire and that was even further away.

It seemed quite a challenge, so with all that in mind, I joined the committee.

We used to meet once a month, at the soon to be elected club presidents house in Josselin. The first meetings were held through the autumn and winter, there were just a handful of us at this time, but we hoped things would pick up come the spring. We used these meetings to plot and plan, to nurture ideas and to drink wine. As spring approached, things did indeed start to gain momentum, there were a few more responses to our request for players, from the expat websites. We were in discussions, with two Maires for possible pitch venues. And most important of all, we had our first game booked, away at Des Ormes in April.

Our committee became all proper. We had a President, only fair as he was the founder and key driving force of the project, and we used his house for our meetings. We had a secretary, a treasurer, and a captain; me! When the role came up for election, I happened to mention I had done it before, and that was good enough for everyone, and I was duly elected.

As spring approached, the possibility of more good news reached our ears. A Marie at a village called Quilly, a small commune about twenty minutes from Josselin, was considering letting us play on their old football pitch. But first we had to fulfil our obligations as a sports club, and provide them with our insurances, our association registration documents and any other relevant paperwork. In our excitement of setting up the club we had forgotten the French obsession with paperwork. It was at this point dealing with the insurances and registration that we realised the club didn't have a name. We didn't really know where our home ground was going to be, so Josselin nomads seemed a good call. Then someone came up with Club Cricket d l'Oust, it was quite the mouthful, but l'Oust was a river that ran here, there, and everywhere in our region. So, it was figured wherever we ended up, it would be near that river. Now we had a name, it made progress with the paperwork a bit easier.

While this was progressing, our first game loomed near, and as the day got nearer, prospective players one by one dropped out. It was being left to us six on the committee to provide the backbone of the team. At home I encouraged and then insisted that Jack and Harry play, despite never playing cricket in their life. And as luck would have it, we had friends over for a visit that weekend, so that was two more players to the cause. They seemed quite keen and up for the challenge, despite also, never having a cricket ball bowled in anger at them. On the sixteenth of April 2006, Club Cricket de l'Oust strode out for their first game. Des Ormes batted first, and showing no sympathy against a team consisting of 50% novices, rattled up 232 runs and we were skittled out for 59. I was second top scorer with nine! We were to learn later that with Des Ormes it was all about the win, and they were known for getting in "ringers." These were ex county players, semi-professional players, etc. It was win at all costs for Des Ormes.

Our next game was in May, away to Gourin, this team had been formed by the four French lads, that had been at the first meeting I attended. They had formed a team, from them four, and expats that lived in their surrounding area. As for the game, we managed to improve our batting and were all out for eighty-eight runs. We had them struggling on 21 runs for 7 wickets and were on course for a comfortable victory, when the scourge of all cricket matches intervened and it rained. The match was declared a draw. A few weeks later in the following rematch, we were soundly beaten, after being bowled out for just forty-two runs.

Our enquiries had revealed the existence of another cricket team, about two hours' drive from us. They were called La Moulin, and they invited us down for a match in June. The day came and we made the long journey down to their ground. On arrival, we noticed they had a nice set up, a decent pitch and even a pavilion. More worrying on meeting the team, you couldn't help but notice that this was a young, athletic team, they must have all been in their early twenties. This could be a tough one, was the general concern among our players. La Moulin batted first, and we restricted them to 177 runs for nine wickets. It is worth noting here, that after just a couple of games, Harry had started to show good skills as a bowler. This was his first game to have a bowl in match conditions, and he took 4 wickets for 35 runs – not bad. I managed to chip in with three wickets for 15 runs. At tea, thoughts and mutterings turned to the long drive ahead of us, and as to what time we would in fact get home. We needn't have worried we were all out for 29 and soon on our way home.

It was during this first summer, that the Marie at Quilly came through for us. We had provided all the necessary paperwork and had received the seal of approval. The old football pitch was ours to use, as soon as the farmer had removed his sheep. Once this had happened, a committee scouting party went to have a look. The initial findings were that once, we have cleared and levelled all the mole hills, cleared up all the sheep dung and run a mower round. It might just work; we could have our pitch. Work parties were arranged and the search for someone with a decent tractor mower began. Although the Marie did help out with the initial grass cuts, and we soon had a field on which could be held a game of cricket.

A home game was arranged for us to take on Gourin at Quilly. It was a good competitive game, and at last we ran out winners, scoring 82 runs to Gourins 42. And several cars were seen to stop, and marvel and wonder what sort of strange ritual was being played out, by these men in white, in the middle of the Brittany countryside. It was our first victory, but our joy was slightly tainted by the realisation that we had no facilities at our ground. No toilets, no washing area, no running water, nothing really. Although Quilly would do for now, we needed to carry on our search for something better.

There soon followed another home game, this time against the youngsters of La Moulin. And as expected they dished out another hiding.

Our next home game was against a touring orchestra, who liked to play a bit of cricket on the side. They had heard of us by the power of the internet, made contact and a game was hastily arranged. This game gave us our

second victory. The game was played in a good spirit, they were a great bunch of lads, and the fixture was made a permanent event for every year. There soon followed another touring team, but this time there wasn't a trumpet in sight, this was a proper cricket team. This was a keenly fought contest, but we fell short, and the tourists run out winners. We finished the season off with two games in consecutive weeks against our old foes, Gourin. We were starting to show some end of season form and won both games.
We finished our first season having played 10, drawn 1, lost 5 and won 4. On reflection we were quite happy with this, as at the start of the season half our team had never played before.

As the year was coming to an end and Christmas drew near. We decided to hold a Christmas party and awards night. It was a good turnout, and everyone was buzzing about the season that had just gone and looking forward to a new one ahead. We had a full fixture list, sponsors and had been given a new ground, complete with sports hall for training. It also had toilets, showers and most importantly a bar area, for us to stock and use. The sports hall would be available to us one evening a week, for training during the year, but especially good, was that we could keep our eye in with batting and bowling practice during the close season, even if it was with a rubber ball. As for the awards, Jack won the Most Improved Player, and I was lucky enough to get the Player of the Year award. No fiddles here, the awards were all voted for by the rest of the team.

The new year began, and we started to use our new training facility. Our new ground was at a town called Serent, this was further away than Quily, about a half hour drive from home. We had been given permission to use the football pitch when the football season was over. Our new ground was definitely a step up, we had toilets, a car park, and the bar area, where we could present our teas from and sell beer. We were starting to feel like a proper team especially as our new team shirts had arrived, complete with team name and club sponsor written on them.

Fully fit and trained up? The season started with a few school cricket demonstrations. It had always been an objective to introduce the game to the locals and these school demos seemed an ideal way of doing this. The French students seemed to struggle with the whole concept of the game but took to it with that youthful exuberance. Although the game did earn some respect when they found out how hard the ball was. A memory that stands out the most for me during one of these mock games, was I had positioned myself as wicketkeeper behind the stumps. A lad came in and bowled a surprisingly straight ball, the student batting gave an almighty swing and amazingly contacted with the ball. The ball went straight up for some distance, and then as it would, gravity took over and the ball came straight down. The batsman hadn't moved from his spot and was looking around at his mates seeking their praise for actually hitting the ball. As the ball hurtled towards him, he mistook their warning shouts as cheers of praise. The ball came down and hit him hard – on the head. Despite being offered a helmet for protection, the lad had declined. We should have insisted! I thought to myself, this isn't going to look good for the club. I could see the headlines now, 'Schoolboy killed in cricket demonstration game, playing of cricket banned while investigations take place' But somehow the lad remained standing and if anything was a little embarrassed by the attention he was now getting. After all the checks he didn't even to appear to have slight concussion, that boy must have had one hard head. We carried out about half a dozen of these school demonstrations; they passed off without further incident, although we did insist the batsman wore a helmet. They were considered a great success by all those who attended, especially us, as we managed to avoid, any unwelcome headlines.

The season began with a trip, to play as we were to nickname them, the 'ringers' at Des Ormes. I don't have the result, but I guess we would have lost. I don't have the facts and figures for our games in 2007, but it was a busy season. The highlights of the year were a couple of weekend tours away. The first was to a six a side tournament played over two days at Des Ormes. In the true spirit of the game and as expected, the 'ringers' invited over from the UK a couple of ex-county players to help them with their cause. Despite that, it was a good weekend, the Des Ormes pitch is on a vast lavish campsite with some superb amenities. There were swimming pools, many other sporting activities, bars, and a nightclub. The only blot on the weekend was when one of the Gourin players thumped one of the La Moulin players for chatting up his daughter. This aside a great weekend was had by all, not sure who won the tournament, but I could have a guess.

The other weekend tour was an expedition down to the Loire and the Vendee. On the Saturday we would be playing Saumur, who boasted of having Mick Jagger as their club president. Apparently, he had a house nearby and had even been known to play a game or two. The ground was in the Loire valley, right by the river, and as befits the area, was in a beautiful location, with a fairy tale chateau looking over it from its lofty perch.

We stayed on a nearby campsite with a few other families. After the long drive and setting up our tents, we all hit the swimming pool and found we had it to ourselves. It was a nice size pool, with a couple of small flumes and with no lifeguard present, we took it on ourselves to break every rule that were shown in pictures on the 'interdit' poster. The campsite had a curfew of no noise after 10.30 pm, but it did have an area away from the pitches with a small bar and an area where even when the bar shut, you could sit and talk and laugh into the early hours. Which we did. The next morning, we had a visit from the camp Kommandant, who gave us a bollocking for filling up the bins with beer cans and wine bottles!

As for the game, I can't remember the result, although there was no Mick Jagger on view this day. I think it would be fair to say that we lost, they did take their cricket seriously, and we hadn't done ourselves any favours with our pre-match activities. The match and the day passed us by, without any incident, and we headed back to the campsite. After a visit to the pool, it was decided that we would spend the evening by our tents, having a drink. After all, we didn't want any more lectures about filling the litter bins up with litter! We sat round in a circle chatting about the game and the days experiences. We managed to keep the noise down and were generally behaving ourselves when the camp Kommandant appeared. She questioned us as to why we weren't drinking at the bar, probably concerned that the takings weren't going to be as good as last night. We challenged her about the comments about the bin, gave her short thrift and sent her on her way.

It was probably just as well, we didn't have a late session, as we were up early in the morning to take our tents down and pack up all our gear for a trip to the Vendee for our next game. This was another long journey, and we arrived at the pitch at around lunchtime. After the picturesque ground at Saumur this was the polar opposite. The cricket pitch was crammed into the corner of a vast play park, that was surrounded by houses and high-rise blocks. Someone was heard to quip, "it will be just like playing at the Oval." We met our opponents, who were the worst of expat types – arrogant, surly, and almost rude. We were then introduced to the club president, who was the rudest, surliest, and most arrogant of them all. He was full of self-importance and made himself the centre of attention. He was to open the batting and bowling, he was the main umpire, a totally cheaty one at that. And when he was bowling, if he could have bowled and then run up the other end to keep wicket, I think he would have. For all his bravado he wasn't the best of players, and when batting he was soon in trouble and was quite clearly run out. But he refused to go, and went into full tantrum mode, about him being president, it was his club, and it just wasn't fair. Feeling slightly embarrassed and awkward we let him stay. It didn't last much longer as he was clean bowled and couldn't argue that one. We then proceeded to bowl them out quite cheaply.

After their innings and before ours started, there was the traditional cricket tea. The Vendee as is the normal and polite thing to do hadn't catered for us. We had nothing, so just sat around watching our opposition tucking into their food. Our tempers and adrenalin up, we made short work of getting the necessary runs for victory. No sooner had this been accomplished, we were in our cars and on the long journey home. Needless to say, we didn't bother making that trip again.

Another season came to an end and at the Christmas awards party, the family came out quite well. Harry took the Most Improved Player award; his bowling was coming on a treat. Kerry received the Presidents Cup, for her service to the club in providing delicious teas for our home games. And I picked up the trophy for the best bowler. It had been a good year.

The 2008 season came, and we were going from strength to strength. The fixture list was healthy, also word had got round, and we had more touring teams from the UK coming over to play us. I don't have all the fixture statistics for that year, only that we played 14 games, won 6, lost 5, and drew 2. We even started rubbing shoulders with celebrities, one of the touring sides had royal correspondent Jenny Bond, in the wife's entourage. And it turns out, one of our new players had been in an episode of Father Ted.

Among the memorable moments from that year are, someone came up with the brilliant idea that we should play the football team whose ground we shared, at football and then cricket. Amazingly they accepted, and we played the football match first. As expected, we were getting a hammering but managing to keep the score to six: nil. As we entered the last minute, we were awarded a dubious penalty, I think by this time the Ref had taken pity on us. The penalty was put away and the game ended 6: 1. The day was finished off with food and of course, booze and was passed off as a great success. The following week, it was our turn to host and hopefully exact revenge. The football team, as all French do, look at the game of cricket with mixed interest. We gave them a few practice goes with bat and ball and a brief run-down of the rules. They gave the game newfound respect when they realised the level of skill required, and as with all newcomers just how hard the ball is. Being sportsman they had a good eye for the ball and gave it a good go. But our experience and skill saw us win comfortably. There then followed a traditional cricket tea and booze. It was agreed that both events had been greatly received by both teams and new friends made. It was a great result all round.

One beautiful summers afternoon and as the sun beat down on the men dressed in white. We were fielding when suddenly one of the lads in the outfield shouted,
"Oi, they're after the beer!"
Two unknown teenage lads, about 16 years old, who had been hanging around the bar, seized an opportunity to reach over the bar, grab a case of beer each, and make a run for it. The warning shout alerted the whole team, who left their fielding positions to give chase. Headed by the faster, younger players we closed in on the beer rustlers. Who were struggling to run, carrying the weight of the case of beers. It must have looked quite the site to see two teenagers being chased by about a dozen guys all dressed in white. Tiredness set in with the beer bandits and we were getting closer. Suddenly they stopped, and carefully put down the beers, raised their hands in some sort of apology signal and ran off. Our beer recovered, we let them go and returned to the match.

The last game of the season saw us win our first proper trophy. The game ended with mixed emotions, happy that we had won, but sad as this was to be the last game, for myself, Jack, and Harry, as we would be returning back to the UK soon. We had been with the club for three years and seen it grow from strength to strength and had some great experiences and had made many good friends along the way.

At the end of season awards, and in our absence, Harry picked up the Most Improved Players trophy and I got the Bowler of the Year. Happy days.

Before I leave the cricket, the club had a strange invitation this year. Would we be interested in fielding a crew for the annual Dragon Boat event, as we were a recognised sports club now. Apparently, this invite was offered exclusively to the regions sports clubs. Our club president thought it would be a good idea to accept, it would do our standing and prestige a bit of good and put cricket more on the map. I wasn't convinced.
This became more so when I found out the rules of this nautical event. It was held at a large lake, the crew consisted of six rowers, someone on the rudder and the bravest member of the team, standing on a platform at the front of the boat. Armed with a jousting pole, it was their job to push or jab their opponent off the platform, into the water!
The boats would set off from opposite sides of the lake and row towards each other. While the jousters prepared themselves, the lance was pretty much what you would expect it to be, apart from the tennis ball stuck on the pointy end, to restrict serious damage. The jouster had on a chest protector which was supposed to be the target zone. As more and more team members found out this information, so more and more team members dropped out.

The day of the event neared, and the only takers were, the President, there was no way he was getting out of it, after all it was he, who had accepted the invitation. Then there was me, Kerry, Jack, Harry, and Maggie, who we thought could man the rudder. And for good measure I had roped in a neighbour and my friend Eddie, who foolishly, over a couple of beers agreed to be the jouster. I told him not to worry, it will be a laugh.

We also got to hear through the grape vine, that the local teams were looking forward to giving the English a good soaking.

On the day, we embraced our unpopularity, by stringing up the Jolly Roger at the back of the boat. And as we set off across the water, we set up a kind of Viking tribal chant in beat with the rowing rhythm. As we neared our opponents the jeers and boos aimed at us from the spectator's bankside, increased in volume. The jousters tussled but neither could be shifted, and our first event was declared a draw.

An hour or so later and we were off again, our ears ringing to the sound of boos and jeers. This time as we made contact there was a clash of oars, the rule was that you pulled them in as the jousters made contact. Both sides were at fault, but not really surprising, was the judge's decision that it was down to us, and we were disqualified. We decided to take our punishment on the chin, as we had had enough of this silly sport anyway, rolled up the Jolly Roger and left, agreeing to stick to cricket.

I would like to dedicate this cricket section to those that were connected to the club and that are no longer with us. Especially Jon, (AKA El Presidente and Tumbleweed, because of his ability to tell poor jokes) one of the key instigators and motivators of the whole Club Cricket de l'Oust journey and club president. Also, Jack, the bearded fellow, who had invited me into his home on that first meeting, who along with Jon, over a few beers, had first had the idea of forming the team.

And Tariq, scorer and umpire extraordinaire, great team supporter, and an extra special thanks, for taking the boys under his wing, especially Harry, in teaching them the rudiments of the game. R.I.P guys.

Chapter Eleven

Back to our first year of living in Brittany, that first summer was passing by nicely, the weather was good, we were exploring our new surroundings and generally enjoying life. But September came, and reality hit the kids with a bang, when school term started. We had done the necessary interviews and form filling, and so Jack was to start at the Madame de Sevigne college in nearby Mauron, about 10km away. He wasn't best pleased when he was told he would have to redo, what I would call, his first year at big school again, because of his lack of French. Which was proved and rubbed in, when his teacher after introducing him to his new class, asked him in front of everyone,
"Ou est ton nez"
Jack looked at her blankly, so she asked again, Jack shrugged and said,
"I don't understand."
"Where is your nose" replied the teacher, in perfect English.
And with that the whole class burst into laughter, an interesting introduction to French school life.

Harry and Maggie were to go to the local school in Guilliers. They did have the reassurance of having each other's support, and in a school of about one hundred pupils there were now ten English children. The local Marie and the school were more than happy with this as it gave them the numbers to keep the school open.
All seemed well for the first term, they were probably experiencing that new kid celebrity status. And for now, the teachers were being quite lenient with them, and they were starting to pick up the French language. Although in Harrys memory he says he spent the first year at this

school playing games on the computer. Obviously, there were new things to get used to, like at Harry and Maggies school, there was one set of toilets for the use of both boys and girls. The girls had to walk past the urinals to get to the 'traps,' Maggie thought this was most disgusting. One thing that took me back to my school days, was the teachers practice of throwing chalk at pupils who were chatting or not paying attention. A nastier practice that horrified Maggie, was her teachers' habit of smoking one of those awful strong French cigarettes, while she was sitting at his desk reading to him. It created a nasty smell and haze over the whole reading experience. At least Harrys teacher had a bit more respect, as in moments of anger and stress, he would go and stand outside the classroom door and puff furiously on his pipe, filling the corridor up with acrid smoke.

As autumn, came and the temperatures started to drop. Harry took to wearing his army style balaclava to school. This balaclava had two eyeholes and hole for the mouth, but this item of clothing was responsible for our first letter home, from a school. This letter gave us a minor ticking off. It asked that we didn't let Harry wear that balaclava to school anymore, as it was frightening the younger children.

The first term came to an end and with Christmas in sight, they broke up from school. We enjoyed our first Christmas in France, and everything seemed fine. But when term started again in January, it wasn't long before things started to get tough. The honeymoon period was over. School became harder as the kids learnt, they had to strive towards getting the marks, they would need to move up to the following year. Don't make the grade and you are held down and must re-do the school year. All three kids suddenly had a downer on their life in France and it affected us all. The Brittany winter wasn't helping, it was cold and wet most days, and on days that it wasn't, it was cold and foggy. Things got so bad towards the end of that first winter, I feel had we not sold our house in the UK, we would have moved back. But as we didn't have the luxury of that safety net, the kids didn't have much choice than to stick at it. And stick at it they did, their French improved, as did the weather and all our moods. Crisis averted.

They were adjusting to French school culture too. Harry and Maggie had Wednesday afternoon off, but had to go in Saturday morning, although this practice was stopped while we still lived there. They had two hours for school dinners, as of course is the French way. Harry and Maggie had to leave the school every lunchtime and walk, two by two up to the centre of the village to the canteen. Their thoughts on their lunchtime experience differ here. Maggie says the dinners were quite nice, although they were, very much of the eat what your given or go without type of dinners. Harrys memory points more to the canteen staff, who he claims were the scariest, meanest people in France, who spent most of the time shouting and screaming at all the children. At Jacks college the canteen was on site, and it was the same two-hour break. The meal consisted of three courses, starter was something like coleslaw, gherkins, pate, and cheese. Followed by either pasta, ratatouille, chips, mash or green beans and meat or fish. Dessert could be anything from ice cream, a yoghurt or apple tart. Accompanying the meal was as much bread and water as you wanted. If during the meal you ended up with something you didn't want, you simply held up your plate inviting another student to take it.

The first school year came to an end, and Jack was disappointed to find out he was going to be held down, to do that year again. The school said that although his French was coming on very well, it still wasn't good enough for the intense learning required of a student at college. That would mean, Jack doing the first year of big school three times, one in the UK and two in France. Harry and Maggies schooling weren't as intense, and they were progressing fine.

As all their language skills improved, school became just school, some good times, and some bad times.
Sport became more of an interest, and moved on from Harrys early description, of PE at the Guilliers school. He said it used to be standing in the small hall or if it wasn't raining, standing in the playground. You would be given a hula hoop and told to get hula hooping. If you messed about or failed miserably at the said task, apparently it wasn't uncommon to see a hoop being bounced of a child's head, as Maggie could testify. At college, Jack was following in the family tradition of being a good distance runner. He won his years cross country race and later on in his school life, had victories in regional and departmental events. His school was very proud of him, as were we, and he came within a whisker of representing them in the nationals and then who knows – France.

Harry's career as a distance runner came unstuck at the first attempt, he finished down the field but explained later that eating six croque monsieur's for lunch before the race, probably wasn't the best preparation.

All three of the kids did sailing as part of the curriculum in their first year at college. This took part on the local lake at Mauron. All the students had their own one person sailing dinghy, and as they drifted across the lake bumping into each other, the teacher tried to keep control by barking instructions through a megaphone, as she sailed alongside them in her own little dinghy.

When one by one, they reached the second year of college, they had the opportunity to go on a week's skiing in the French Alps. The trip was subsidised by the school, it would have been a crime not to let them go and experience this. As Harry said in his own words "we had such an incredible time on the slopes, my pal and me, that we hatched a plan to flunk the rest of the year, so we would be held down and could go skiing again."
Harrys pal was a lad called Maro and came from Madagascar. He came into Harrys class but being foreign and black, he struggled to make friends among the local kids. Harry seeing his plight, let him join his work group, where upon one of the other kids said, "if my parents knew I was working with a black kid, they would be very angry."
But undeterred and fair play to Harry, he didn't let things like this bother him, and he and Maro became best friends. Unfortunately, this marked Harry and Maro out as foreigners and they became the target for the school bullies. One-time Maro, had tippex poured on his head by one of them, to try and make him white! The bullying did follow them on their skiing trip, but it didn't dampen their enthusiasm for a return visit.

I'll let Harry tell you about this part in his own words,
"Year 8"
"Back to skiing for another epic trip. This year as we had been held down, we didn't have to go through the same bullying as last year. We had a much easier time in the evenings as me and Maro shared a room. We were in the top group for skiing, due to experience gained from the

previous year. So we were on the harder slopes, which were amazing. We were able to watch a snowboarding show one evening, which was fantastic. And I don't know if it was because we were a bit older, but we were also allowed into the village in our spare time. The only downer on this trip, was that this years' psycho had managed to buy himself a knife and stabbed up his mattress and bedding. And the teachers thought putting him in with us would be the best way forward. The first thing he did in his dark rage was throw all our clothes out the window. Then stabbed up our beds! The whole feeling of safety had gone again. Luckily, he was a psycho and not a bully, so in a strange way he was easier to manage."

As well as the skiing there were endless school trips and days out, some were educational some were just for fun. One such educational trip was for a friends daughter who was in the ballet club. Every year they used to take a coach, up to Paris to watch one of the prestige shows, like Swan Lake. Every year, the coach would fill up with young, excited girls, the age range was from four to eleven, and then there would be the long-suffering teacher and helpers. And every year the girls would be chatting, dancing, singing and generally being excitable all the way up in the coach. Then fall asleep in the performance and then mess about all the way home.

One trip that Harry and Maggie went on was supposed to be a mixture of fun and historical fact. The trip was to Puy du Fou, which modestly referred to itself as the best theme park in the world. Puy du Fou was a very long drive away, so it meant an early start, a very early start, and a late, very late finish. It was a big ask to do it all in a day, but the kids thoroughly enjoyed it. The day was packed with stunt filled re-enactments of Romans v the

Gaul's, Vikings fighting anyone, and of course those lifelong enemies, the French v the English, in their many wars throughout the ages. And of course, the French won all these skirmishes.

On the subject of history, the kids relayed some interesting facts they had learnt in their history lessons at school. How the French, single handedly won both world wars? Napolean was this great, amazing guy – the saviour of France. Only his victories were discussed, no mention of the deaths and misery, he caused mainly to his own people. No mention of abandoning his army in Egypt or the defeat at Waterloo. There was also no place for Crecy, Agincourt, or the Battle of Trafalgar in the French curriculum. Over dinner, one evening Jack casually mentioned,
"I learnt something new today, my teacher reckons Jesus was French."
After nearly choking on my peas, I laughed and thought, just what are these teachers teaching them these days.

I mentioned that Harry experienced bullying, Jack seemed to predominately escape this nasty behaviour, but unfortunately Maggie wasn't so lucky. Maggie had a major issue with bullying at her first school, that little sweet school in Guilliers. This was no racially motivated bullying either, as the lad in question, who I shall call Dudley, was English. Maggie used to tell us what Dudley got up to, how like all bullies he picked on those weaker than himself, younger girls were his favourite target. Maggie told us he was always pinching, punching, and pulling the younger girls hair. Initially, we put it down to playground bickering and telling tales. But after Harry had moved on to college, without him there to look after her, things for Maggie got worse and the bruises and marks started to appear on her. And the younger girls were having their snack stolen by Dudley and if any objected, he reacted violently. One girl was swung around by her pig tails and let go. It was only after talking to other parents with daughters at the school we realised how bad the problem was. The concerned parents agreed something must be done, so it was decided we would all see the principle at separate meetings and bring this situation to his attention. The principle seemed unimpressed with all our reports and so accordingly was going to do nothing about it. We were later to find out that this reason for lack of care, was that he was good pals with Dudleys father, and they would spend most Saturday evenings together drinking and smoking a little exotic tobacco.

Dudleys reign of terror continued, Maggies arms and legs often had bruises on them. We felt powerless to do anything about it, and to be fair to Maggie she wasn't making a major fuss over it, at this stage. One night I picked Maggie up from school and she was particularly stressed. Apparently, Dudley was taking one of the smaller girls sweets and she had got very upset about it, Maggie seeing what was going on, tried to intervene. Dudley had taken exception and strangled Maggie, and she still had the red marks on her neck. Still the principle refused to act.

One night Maggie came home terribly upset, when we spoke to her about what was up. She broke down and told us, Dudley had brought some porno mags into school and was forcing all the girls to look at them, telling them that's what your mum and dad get up to every night. And then to top it off, he tried to put his hand down Maggies top. When she resisted and struggled, he thumped her and strangled her.

We decided that if the school wasn't going to do something about it, we must. This had gone too far and gone on too long. We kept her out of lessons and started looking for a new school for her. This didn't prove to be much of a problem, and we soon had a place secured for her at a school in Mauron. The place reserved, Kerry, Maggie and I marched into the school and demanded a meeting with the principle. He was halfway through a lesson and refused to see us, we were pretty insistent and reluctantly he came out to meet us. We stood there in the playground and told him the recent events regarding Dudleys bullying, he still didn't seem to be bothered and even at one point, gave the gallic shrug. Realising we weren't getting anywhere, and he wasn't going to take any action. We told him we were going to do something about it, and we were going to be changing Maggies school. Hearing this, his mood and tone changed, we did hear later that if a student changes school for anything other than moving house, it can look bad on the principle, and the school, and questions are asked. He said he would start to take our accusations seriously and then rambled on a lot. Not convinced, we told him that we would leave the decision to Maggie. The principle towered over her and spoke.
"Well Maggie, is changing school what you want."
Avoiding the attempt at intimidation, she looked him back and said,
"Yes, I do"
Not bad for a nine-year-old, she never went back to that school again. She started her new school straightaway and started to rebuild and enjoy school life again.

The story of Dudleys bullying doesn't end there. Two of the young girls that he used to pick on, were daughters of friends of ours, my cycling buddy Eddie, and his wife Tanya. Tanya had a son from a previous marriage –

Dennis, who lived in England with his dad. He came over for frequent visits in the school holidays and being about the same age as Jack and Harry, they had struck up a friendship.

On one such trip and annoyed with Dudleys treatment of their sisters, they began scheming and plotting. At this point I would like it noted that none of the adults were aware of what they were up to. Apparently, the plan was to cycle over to his house, Harry would go and call for Dudley while Jack and Dennis would carry on down the lane and lie in wait for him. Harry was to lead Dudley down the lane, whereupon the other two would jump out, surprising their prey. They would hold him down and spray his hair, bright yellow with joke party hair spray, all the time advising him to leave the girls alone.

That was the plan, but reality is a different thing. The chosen day arrived, and they met up and cycled over to Dudleys. Harry went to call for him while the other two hid up. It wasn't long before Harry and Dudley came walking down the lane, so far so good. As they approached Dennis and Jacks hiding place, the pair of them jumped out. At first Dudley was surprised and froze, but he quickly gained his composure and produced a large knife from within his coat. The sort of knife Crocodile Dundee or Rambo would be familiar with. He gripped the knife with both hands and waved it towards them. Dennis thinking this had gone a bit too far, tried to make light of it before someone got seriously hurt and produced his keyring, which has a small novelty pen knife attached to it. The sort of thing you would get out of a Christmas cracker. Dennis started adopting some crazy kung fu positions, with a kind of martial art shout as he went. Jack and Harry started to laugh and Dudley seizing his opportunity ran off.

"Oh no!" shouted Harry, "he will get his dad!"
Dudleys dad just happened to be a six foot plus ex squaddie. Fearing the repercussions Jack and Dennis jumped on their bikes and shot off.
"Oi, wait for me" said Harry, regretting his decision to leave his bike at Dudleys house. As expected Dudleys dad turned up at the ambush point and wasn't best pleased. He shouted at Harry,
"Which way did they go."
It seems he was more interested in them, than Harry.
"They went that way" said a relieved Harry, pointing in the wrong direction. Dudleys dad stormed off, leaving Harry to go and retrieve his bike, and head for home. When he got home, he found Jack and Dennis hiding in the garden. And gave them a piece of his mind for being abandoned. They had a bit of a shouting match, but soon calmed down and agreed it had ended the best way – considering.
The next Sunday morning, there was a battering on the front door and there through the glazed panels stood the ominous figure of Dudleys dad. I had just been on my usual Sunday morning bike ride and was tucking in to my well-earned fry up. I went to the door, opened it, and was told,
"I need to speak to you now, outside."
Bloody hell, now what? am I about to get my arse kicked? After all he was about two foot taller than me. We moved away from the house, and I braced myself. There was a lot of raised voices, and sometimes shouting but thankfully no violence. Of course, the main subject of this conversation was Dudleys behaviour at school, but I'd like to think I gave as good as I got. The conversation ended abruptly, and he left. I went indoors and announced to Kerry,
"Well, that's us off their Christmas card list."
I returned to my now cold breakfast – great!

I'm not sure if this is when we found out what the boys had been up to, but we soon were.

While I was at work on the Monday, my mobile rang and I had an angry and agitated Kerry, on the line. When she had calmed down, she told me that,
"The gendarmes have been in touch, there has been a complaint made against Jack, Harry, and Dennis. Daddy Dudley had been to the local gendarmerie and reported the boys for jumping Dudley and threatening to stab him. A request had been made for the boys to attend the station on Wednesday afternoon. Dennis however, avoided this appointment as he had returned to the UK, that very day.

So, for the first time in our lives, we found ourselves at a police station, helping them with their enquiries. We all had to give individual statements, in French of course. When it came to Maggies turn, she told the whole sorry and disturbing saga of Dudleys bullying at school. The officer could hardly believe what was being told to him, if Dudleys behaviour wasn't bad enough, he couldn't believe that the school turned a blind eye to it. He thanked us for the information and said that there would be no further action taken against the boys. He said he would be talking to the school, and particularly the principle. He also said he would be calling Dudley and Dudley Snr, in for a formal appointment. And that, was that we were free to go.

With Maggie away from the school, we never had anything more to do with Dudley and his family ever again. We never did find out if they suffered any legal repercussions,
It was probably, just a bollocking and a warning. A couple of years later at a social event, we were

approached by Maggies former principle, who apologised for his part in not being stronger in dealing with the whole Dudley bullying saga.

Moving on from this but still focusing on the kids school life, we were all pleased and proud when Jack passed his Brevet. A diploma awarded to students allowing them to leave college and go to a Lycée, which is for higher education and could be trade based, if desired. Jack fancied the idea of being an engineer, and particularly an aircraft technician. We managed to find a Lycée that covered this, contacted them, and gave over some of Jacks details. Interested, they asked him in for a chat, despite being over a three-hour drive, we set off. It was a quite informal interview and while they were quite impressed with Jack, they did stress however it was quite difficult to get a place there as they only had thirty places, and that was for the whole of France. Getting the message, we started to search for something a little closer.

We managed to find a Lycée that catered for the aspiring engineer, just outside the medieval town of Dinan, about forty minutes' drive away. He attended the interview and was promptly offered a place. Although reasonably close to home, he would be expected to board there from Monday to Friday. He wasn't struck on the idea, but we spent most of our time trying to convince him these would be the best years of his life, making new friends, the parties, and the laughs. Memories that would stay with him for the rest of his life.

On his first morning, his bags all packed, Kerry and I drove him to the Lycée and the start of his new adventure. As we went through the gates, a large, grey sinister building loomed up in front of us. A bit like a wing of Colditz, I thought but kept it to myself. We said our goodbyes and he said, he would ring us that night with an update. Well, he certainly did and unleashed a barrage of anger. His room was like a prison cell, and he shared with two other lads who hated him already. There was 9.00 PM curfew, and it was lights out at 9.30PM. You could only leave the building before nine and that was only if you were a smoker and wanted a last one before bedtime. The lights came back on at 6.30AM. There was a warden on every floor keeping order, and mealtimes were a horrible, regimented affair. It's like being in prison, was his final comment. I don't think he was totally happy with his new adventure.

We put it down to first day nerves and anxieties and said we would be better prepared next week. We would sort him out a laptop or portable DVD player so at least he could watch movies in the evenings. And perhaps a radio so he could listen to some tunes.

The next nights phone call was no better, he had enquired about having a laptop or similar in his room and was told in no uncertain terms that this was forbidden. Also, his roommates had joined forces and were being complete tits towards him. And another nail in the coffin of this great adventure, was that it turns out this course was to train people to be machinists in a factory, not what any of us had in mind at all. Something must have got lost in translation, this was no engineering course.

The next day while I was at work, Kerry rang to tell me that Jack had been on the phone. He was very unhappy; he didn't want to do this anymore and it wasn't how he saw his life mapping out for the next three years. Kerry and I both agreed, let's get him out of there. Kerry got off the phone to me and text Jack, "Pack your bags, I'm on my way."

Kerry waited in the Lycée car park and at lunchtime Jack appeared with his bags and textbooks. He got in the car; Kerry took his books off him and went to see the principle. She knocked on the door and not waiting for a reply walked in, the principle looked up from her paperwork, but before she could speak, Kerry in her best French said.

"Bonjour, I'm Jack Brewers mum, these are his textbooks, I'm taking him home now and he won't be coming back, Au Revoir."

With that Kerry spun round and headed out of the office, leaving a stunned principle who had not managed to say a word during this minor invasion of her office.

Kerry contacted Jacks old school and explained the predicament, they were surprisingly understanding and offered their help and support. And within a couple of days had found him a place on an electrical and electronics course at Josselin, so nice and local. There was no compulsory boarding here, he settled in nicely and was a great deal happier there. Even more so, when the students went on strike and held a protest, blocking up the road. Coming home every night, proper cheered him up, and it wasn't long before he was doing the journey under his own steam, first on a moped and then upgrading to a scooter. Unless it was cold or wet that is, then he would get his mum to take him – bloody lightweight.

I'll finish off this chapter with some of the kids lighter memories of their school life in France.

Harry – went on a school trip to Jersey, on the boat on the way back, someone had the bright idea of spraying

fart spray in a girls mouth, who then proceeded to projectile vomit over the surrounding members of her class. Later on, I tried to cheer her up by swinging on a pole and pretending to fall off.
Then one time I did actually fall off, breaking all the stink bombs I had hidden in my backpack. The smell was terrible, and it stank out the whole seating area. The harassed teacher finding out my bag was to blame, opened the door and threw it out onto the deck, I really thought it was going overboard.

Maggie – Dad coming to school to pick me up on his bicycle, and me sitting on the handlebars, facing him with my hands around his neck, singing all the way home. Also being picked up from school on dads motorbike was epic. I was a hero in front of the other kids. I even had my own little crash helmet and everything.

Jack – Spent an entire lesson with the sports teacher teaching us swimming with one of his bollocks hanging out of his shorts.

Maggie – Learning maths in French, I can't even figure it out in English! Somehow getting a lower grade in music than the French students when the song we had been learning was in English? Being told if I focused more on my classes than my hair, I might actually do something with my life!

Harry – We got to do paintballing with the teachers, just before the exams. It was brilliant! My arch enemy, my FLE teacher (FLE = translates as French language for foreigners) well she was there, and I caught her hiding behind a tree. I snuck up behind her and unloaded a full magazine of paintballs on her butt. She shrieked in pain and fell down the bank. The next day she was at school hobbling around on crutches.

Jack – In science we were given straws which we had to shove into the lungs, that had been removed from some unfortunate rabbit. One of my pals while demonstrating how the lungs expanded, laughed, and sucked instead of blowing, got a mouthful of dead rabbit organs, and promptly threw up.

Harry – Year 4 (year 9 in England) All I remember about this year is the work getting harder but instead of knuckling down and concentrating, I spent the time messing about with Maro. I'm fairly sure we messed about all year, chatting, farting, and generally not caring. Then we would play football in all the hours before, between and after lessons, after school, Wednesday afternoons and weekends. We also had a lesson called FLE (as explained above) It was to help us with the end of year exams. It didn't! Again, we just messed about and one time the teacher, proper lost the plot and ripped up all my work and books. It didn't help that Franco, Maros brother was at that lesson too, and if anything, he was worse especially with the farting. I remember this one time; he was chewing gum while swinging backwards on his chair eyeing up the girl behind. The gum spilled from his mouth, rolled up his face and into his hair. The rest of the lesson was spent trying to extract the gum from his hair.

Jack – A lad thought it would be funny to bring a large dildo to school, that he had found in one of his mums drawers in her bedroom. It would probably have gone unnoticed had he not started hitting fellow students on the head with it, which obviously raised some complaints, and the lad was sent to the principal's office with the offending item. The principle decided he should be sent home, and the whole incident was compounded when it was the mum that had to come and get him and the dildo.

Jack – One time the English teacher was laying into the class about something or other, when one of the French students stood up and said in English.
"Madame, you are full of pudding."

And the last word on French school goes to Harry.
"I didn't pass my exams as expected, but wouldn't change anything about my schooling in France, but rather have the fond memories of the good times."

Chapter Twelve

The branch of our bank was situated in a town called La Trinite Porhoet, a lovely little town with a beautiful church, medieval buildings, and an old wash house, on the bank of the little river running through it. One day on a trip to the bank, there on the grassy mound as we entered the town was a massive poster, saying which translated as, 'coming soon, ham & chips.' Now I'm not saying that not a lot happened round this way, but when it did it was proper supported. Anything with food and drink was guaranteed a full house. Even boot fairs, as well as having the stall holders selling their wares, there were also plenty of food and drink stalls, otherwise no one would have come. We went to a boot fair, early one morning at Guilliers. The two old boys at the gate collecting the entrance fee, were already halfway down a nice bottle of sauvignon blanc. Good lads.

There was a poster campaign round Guilliers advertising a disco and raclette. Interested, first we had to find out what a raclette was, turns out it is a type of cheese. And the meal was to be, this melted cheese poured over ham and new potatoes. We booked some tickets, and it wasn't long before the night out arrived, and off we went to the Foyer Municipal de Guilliers – Guilliers village hall. It was like the whole village had turned up; the hall was packed. We managed to find a table, sat down, and waited in anticipation of the evening ahead. There was no bar, everyone bought their own drinks with them. Before the dancing began, it was food time. I thought it was going to be a bun fight, but it was quite well organised, and we formed orderly queues in our groups. Once you reached the food tables, you were given a plate with boiled potatoes on, you then moved on to be given your portion of ham and then lastly to the raclette. This was a large wheel of cheese and a heater, like the sort you would get in a kebab shop. As you presented your plate, the cheese was cut off as it spun round, again much the same as a kebab. If the cheese was not quite melty enough, you had to wait for a few more turns of the wheel.

Back at the table and tucking into my food, as I looked at the stage it dawned on me that it was hardly set up for a disco. There were no turntables, no massive speakers, and no flashing lights, in fact the stage was quite bare. Perhaps the disco hadn't turned up yet, no urgency, after all this is France. The food was simple but delicious and duly put away, and a few glasses of wine later, we still had no activity on stage to suggest a disco was being set up. I think I detected that the crowd were getting restless. This crowd consisted of young children right through to the oldest gran & grandad. As in most countries in Europe, the family is important, and they do lots of things together as a family unit. Something us Brits seemed to have lost. The buzz of the crowd was growing louder and just when it seemed it could boil over, a man appeared on stage carrying a microphone and stand. The audience satisfied that something could be happening, settled down. The man having set up the mike stand, left the stage and returned with a couple of speakers, the sort that wouldn't look out of place on most people's hi-fi system at home. The man strategically placed the speakers and left the stage. Once again, the crowd grew restless.

As the restlessness was hitting a crescendo, an old feller appeared on stage. He was probably in his seventies, was wearing a tatty old tweed suit with a well-worn flat cap and was carrying a battered old accordion. An accordion,

I thought this was supposed to be a disco. With the large gathering of teenagers there that night, who were obviously expecting to dance to some disco tunes, I feared for the accordionists safety. With no introductions, the accordionist burst into a traditional Breton tune. This is it, I thought, trouble time. But to my surprise, encouraged and led by the teenagers, everyone got up, and formed a massive circle, including us. We all linked hands or rather little fingers and danced around the hall. I say danced, we moved sideways, albeit a little rhythmically, lifting our linked fingers up two times, and then down two times, and so on. No one was left sitting, from the youngest child to the oldest granny, they were all up. It was quite a sight.

Our unknown musician carried on with another five slightly different tunes, but the dance moves remained the same. Then before he collapsed with fatigue, he announced he was having a break. This was warmly received as it meant it was wine time. After about twenty minutes he came back, did the same six tunes, but still everyone got up and did the same dance. This carried on for the rest of the night, but we had a great time. No one seemed to question the absence of a disco or was this how disco translated in this part of Brittany!

A year or so of living in Brittany, it was suggested to us by friends that we join the village pumpkin competition. It was an annual event that consisted of meeting up in the spring, and all competitors being given the same pumpkin seeds, type, and quantity. Oh, and drinking wine. It sounded like fun and could be another good way of integrating with the locals. The competition awarded prizes for the biggest, the prettiest, the best overall collection and the tastiest. This was proved by bringing in a dish for everyone to try. Our seeds planted, we diligently watered, fed and generally cared for the growing plants. Autumn arrived and with it the day of the final. We had a nice little collection but had no idea what our competition rivals had in store. We took our offerings down to the local hall, and went in. There were tables set up along one side, on which the exhibitors were to display their produce. As we set up our display, looking at the other tables, our pumpkins were about standard. We got a drink from the bar, found ourselves a seat with a good vantage point, to observe the rest of the competitors setting up. A guy came in with just the one pumpkin, but it was bought in on a wheelbarrow and needed two people to lift it on to the table, which creaked under the weight. Oh well, there's the prize for the biggest gone. Another fellow walked in with two massive bin bags and proceeded to put a load of vine on the table. He turned round, shrugged, and said, "Nothing grew." This was greeted with laughter from his fellow competitors. The tables were eventually full, and people sat around chatting and sipping wine. This is nice, calm, and tranquil, I thought, it could even be an early night and no hangover.

The judges were independent of the competition and bought in for their expertise in pumpkins. We were to find out later that this was a lot of nonsense; they knew nothing about pumpkins and were open to a bit of small-time bribery. As the evening wore on, and tongues were loosened by the impact of alcohol, we were also to find out, that cheating was widespread and had almost become an acceptable part of the competition. Unaware of these facts, we didn't pick up any prizes in our first year of competition, but we were to stand on the winners rostrum more than once in the following years. The wheelbarrow guy as expected won the biggest pumpkin, and with the other prizes awarded, the music came on and the atmosphere ramped up a notch. The alcohol flowed and it wasn't long before people were dancing on the tables and proper enjoying themselves. The event wrapped up at 5 AM, we had had such a great time and had made many friends. Roll on next year.

Another visit on another evening to this hall, was for a karaoke night. Reading through the list of songs, we soon realised our theory that, there will be lots of English songs. After all, English and American songs, were the most popular in the world; that was not the case here tonight. There were just two English songs on the list, My way and New York, New York by Frank Sinatra. So, once we had done our two songs, we had to spend the rest of the evening, listening to people blasting out bad versions of French pop songs, mainly from French favourite Johnny Hallyday. This guy had been around for ever and the majority of the French loved him, they revered him as the French Elvis. To any keen ear, especially mine, I thought he was pretty awful. This wasn't one of our better nights out, it deteriorated into really bad singers, singing really bad songs. We gave the next karaoke a miss.

We used to use the local Tabac in Guilliers, especially after a day toiling down the lake, or if we had dropped one of the kids off for a club, at the Foyer Municipal. These clubs were usually an hour or so long, and it saved us going home. It was also a great way of improving our French, making new friends, and generally integrating. One time, Maggie was doing a dance club every Tuesday evening. After dropping her off, it was into the Tabac. We got chatting to a guy, who come to refer to us, as his English friends. He was a nice, friendly chap, and it turns out, he was the fire chief for the nearby town of La Trinite Porhoet. He liked to have a couple of beers before he went off on his night shift. He enjoyed our conversations and used to save us a place at the bar. After a few months, the Tabac bar had a new owner, and a couple of weeks into this new management, we were invited to a 'Pot d'amitie,' which translates as a friendship pot. It was away of the new manager introducing herself and welcoming people to the bar. And of course, there would be free food and some free wine. As expected, come the night of the event, the place was bursting at the seams. Anticipating this, we had got there a bit early and claimed a couple of seats. The food and wine flowing, the bar had a right buzz to it. Finding out we were English; we became celebrities to those sitting around us. Things really got going, when a guitar was produced, and a sing song broke out. The guitar was passed around the bar, some knew how to play and some not so good. But everyone joined in with the singing, even us, although we didn't have a clue to the words. But everyone was so pissed by now, it didn't really matter. Thankfully, we managed to avoid showing our lack of prowess as musicians, but again, I don't think anyone would have noticed. Arm wrestling started, in one corner of the room, to much applause. And again, I was relieved when it stayed in that corner, and I didn't have to get involved in the dark art of arm wrestling. The evening came to an end, and we all spilled out onto the street. There then followed much handshaking, kissing and embracing, and we all went our separate ways. It had been great fun.

Most of our socialising was done around friends' houses, and us reciprocating by having gatherings at our place. A couple of memorable soirees were at our lake, yes, we had a lake, which I will talk about more in the next chapter. It is worth a chapter on its own.

The first soiree at the lake was when a few lads and their families from the cricket team, joined us for a night under canvas, and drinks, of course. The few drinks turned into many drinks, and the party turned into a music festival, complete with mosh pit. The lads all stripped to the waist and jumped up and down, bumping into each other, and there you have it, the mosh pit experience. One of the lads shouted out something about getting naked, dropped his trousers and pants and bunny hopped off, as best as he could, with his ankles effectively tied together. He tripped over a tent peg, fell onto the tent, and understandably the tent collapsed. The occupants – the kids, were not best pleased and started to shout out. The nudist had somehow got himself stuck and lay there laughing, with his butt, stuck up in the air. When we too, had all stopped laughing, we mounted a rescue party.

The next night of fun down the lake was for my birthday party. We invited several friends, a mixture of French and English, and gave them the option of pitching a tent and staying the night. The night of the party arrived, and the elements smiled down on us, and gave us a perfect hot, sunny June weekend. The afternoon was spent driving round friends' houses and loading up the trailer with patio furniture, tables, and chairs. Then down the lake setting up tents, the BBQ, the seating area, a massive bonfire, and a bar. Guests started arriving in the late afternoon, those camping the night tended to arrive first, and everyone, mucked in, setting up the tents. By 7 PM all our guests had arrived, the BBQ was in full flow as was the alcohol. After everyone had eaten their fill, the first event of the evening was a game of Bat and Trap. The game is, I think, unique to Kent and played in a pub garden. It is played on a grass strip approximately 20 metres long by 4 metres wide. There are two posts at one end, where the bowler and fielders stand. At the other end of the pitch is the trap, which is basically a rectangular box with a small see saw mechanism and a small, hinged target at the front. The hard rubber ball, a bit like a dogs ball, is placed on one end of the see saw, the batter hits the other end of the see saw. The ball. hopefully rises sufficiently enough, for the batter to hit it between the posts. If the ball doesn't go between the posts the batter is out. The batter can be caught out, if the ball doesn't touch the ground and the fielder is behind the line of the posts. The fielding side have an opportunity to roll the ball back and hit the target. If they hit it, the batter is out, if not, it counts as one run.

These simple rules explained, we attempted to play the game. Two team captains were appointed, and they took it in turns to pick their teams. Everyone joined in, the French had never seen a game like this, but then come to think of it, neither had most of the English, in attendance this night. After a few rule issues, everyone took to the game, and it became a good wholesome contest with good wholesome cheating. As darkness fell, we were still playing, improvising floodlighting with car headlights, torches, and lanterns. The game finally came to an end when a batter took an exuberant swing at the ball, got a top edge, and sent the ball flying into the lake. The fielding team attempted to claim the victory by default, but to keep the peace, the game was declared a draw.

After all this activity, there was a period of sitting around chatting, eating, and drinking. As the clock neared to 2 AM, someone came up with the great idea of having a game of bulldog. Amazingly, once the idea had been shared and translated, everyone agreed to play. So, there we were in the early hours of a balmy summers night,

French and English adults and children playing bulldog. This went on for about an hour, and then people started to hit the brick wall, tiredness, drunkenness, the inability to stand up. They either disappeared off to their tent or with a mixture of warm hugs, kisses and general embracing bid us goodbye, and staggered off up the lane in the direction of the village.

The last thing I remember of the night, was a few of us diehards, sitting around the fire talking cobblers. It felt like I closed my eyes for a brief moment, almost like I blinked and when I opened them, it was to a bright blue sky. Coming to my senses, I surveyed my surroundings, taking in the after-party devastation, that was all around. I noticed there was still some sausages, charring away on the BBQ. Feeling a bit peckish, I walked over to the BBQ and stuffed one of the burnt offerings into my mouth. The fact it was like eating a bit of charcoal didn't deter me and I ate another. It was at this point I heard the sound of heaving and retching. Looking round I noticed, one of my pals was awake and seeing what I was doing, suddenly come over feeling unwell.

The morning was spent tidying up and returning peoples garden furniture. The village bottle bank was filled up and the last of the stragglers, decamped and went home. The land around the lake was cleared up and returned to nature. The only evidence of the festivities was the scorch mark made by the bonfire. Peace and tranquillity returned to the lake.

Chapter Thirteen

As I write this chapter, it is with mixed emotions as the subject, our lake, has just been sold. We had the lake for twenty years; it gave us some good times but also gave us a lot of problems and headaches. The good times were the parties, the kids fishing and boating and sometimes just sitting there enjoying the peace, tranquillity and all the best that nature has to offer. The lake was home to kingfishers, ducks, herons, and all sorts of other birdlife. It was also home to a family of Ragondin, we know them as Coypu. As well as thousands of frogs, toads, and lizards.

The problems at the lake pretty much started straightaway. Unbeknown to us, we had inherited a feud between the previous owner and the neighbouring farmer. When the previous owner put the lake up for sale, the farmer wanted to buy it, but the owner said.
"I would rather give it away than sell it to you."
I'm not sure of any other details of the feud, only that it had rumbled on for many years. Rather than meet us and begin a fresh friendly relationship, the farmer decided to carry on with his grudge. He started with trivial things, like having his labourers carry out works around the perimeter, cutting trees and shrubs and throwing all the cuttings on our land. We didn't let this bother us, we had a big heap of our own developing and just added their stuff to our pile, it would make a good bonfire before too long. Then one day two massive tractor tyres appeared on our land, it was obvious where they had come from. The hedge was still flattened where they had been lifted over from the farmers field. We did think about just putting them back over but decided not to rise to the bait. I enlisted the help of a French pal Gerard,

and we somehow got the massive tyres into his van. We drove to two different dechetteries (tips) but were turned away at both of them, the tyres were so big they were considered industrial waste. Then Gerard said,
"I know where we can get rid of these."
And drove off with new purpose. Eventually we left the road, and headed along a single lane, bumpy track, deep into a forest. I tried to explain that I wasn't happy about fly tipping them. He understood and agreed saying,
"Don't worry, you will see why when we get there"
We drove along this challenging track for a while, negotiating fallen trees, deep water filled ruts and many other hazards. After a few sticky situations we eventually pulled into a clearing and stopped. Gerard turned to me and with a serious tone said,
"Watch out, be careful and stay with me."
Bloody hell, I thought, where has he brought me.
"Come" he said, "let's get the tyres out."
We managed to extract the tyres from the van and wheeled the first one round to the front of the van.
"Push" said Gerard.
And we shoved the tyres down the slope, the tyre crashed through the nettles and brambles for a few metres, then disappeared from sight. It hadn't been obvious when we pulled up, but hidden from sight by the undergrowth was a sink hole. I listened out for the anticipated heavy thud, but none came.
"Wow" I said, "how deep is it."
"No one knows" replied Gerard.
We rolled the other tyre in the same direction, with the same result. I never did hear any thuds, perhaps they are still on their way to the earth's core.

This problem was solved, but still the farmer kept up his petty annoying tactics. And still we chose to ignore them. Aside from the farmer, a new problem had presented itself. When clearing the land of metre high grass, brambles, and weeds of all descriptions. The clearance had revealed over fifty large tree stumps, all cut off at ground level. Great, this messed up our plans for using this grassed area for ball games and parties, and aside from that it didn't look very nice. Funny how no one mentioned that these were lying in wait for us. To create our grassy area these would have to be removed, we would have to dig them out. Over the course of two years, working the odd day, here and there, we took on the challenge. Most stumps took the best part of a day to dig out. Some days I would be on my own, some days with Kerry, and even some days the boys would help. We would dig a large hole around the stump, hopefully revealing all the roots. Once the roots were exposed, they would then be cut. If they were reasonably clean, I would use a chainsaw, if they were muddied up, then it would have to be the axe. Mud and stones are no friend of the chainsaw. Once all the roots were cut, a scaffold tube and a two-metre crowbar were wedged under the stump. A support was then placed under the crowbar and scaffold tube so the law of the lever could be applied. Which usually meant me, bouncing on the non stump end, until there was the satisfaction of a loud snap meaning the stump was released from the earths grip. This would then be rolled out of the way, to be dried out, and then burnt later. The hole would then be filled in, and then we would move on to the next one. It sounds like a straightforward process, but it was bloody hard work, and I was ready for my bed, after a days' work digging a stump out.

One day, we were hard at work clearing stumps, when a tractor towing a large contraption pulled up, and parked on the farm track opposite the lake. The driver got out and started tinkering with the big contraption machine thingy, it had been towing, it really looked like something Professor Pat Pending would have invented. Cars and vans started pulling up, and they pulled barrels out of their vehicles. The barrels were emptied into one end of the machine, there then followed all sorts of strange sounds and smells, flames were seen and a lot of smoke fumes. Curiosity got the better of us and we went over to find out what was being carried out in this strange scene. It turns out the barrels contained cider; the cider was poured in one end and went through the machine being heated up to extreme temperatures. The intense heat came from burning logs. After a while, out of the other end of the machine, several gallons of cider were turned into a bottle of rocket fuel, known as Eau du Vie. This Eau du Vie was nigh on pure alcohol and much revered amongst the locals. It was dangerous stuff; you didn't want to drink too much of it or spill any on your clothes. There was talk that the government wanted to ban it, but there was a lot of opposition, and the general consensus was that it would just drive it underground. A further and equally dangerous spin off from Eau du Vie was Schnapps 44, also known as Liquor 44. This was a drink made at home consisting of a litre of Eau du Vie, 1 large orange stabbed 44 times, 44 sugar cubes and 44 coffee beans. The sugar cubes were placed in the bottom of a Kilner jar, the coffee beans inserted into the stabs in the orange, and then the alcohol poured into the jar. Then the jar must be stored in a cool dark place for, yes you guessed it, at least 44 days. Then its traditional not to decant the drink but to place it on the table in the jar and then ladle it out into the glasses. Got to love a tradition. It also had this mystical power, of turning me into a fluent French speaker or so I thought. One evening round a friend's house, a neighbour presented us with our first experience of '44'. After some glasses, my friend and I started talking to each other in what we

thought was French but none of the French could understand us, and apparently it wasn't English, don't know what it was but we understood each other.
Good stuff.
In the meantime, the farmer was still being a tit! One day I happened to be driving by the lake and noticed the farmer walking around the perimeter with another man. I approached them and asked what was going on, and could I be any help, as they were obviously looking and pointing at the lake. They politely ignored me and walked on, I followed and again asked the same questions. Again, they walked on, my French wasn't that good, so I didn't persevere and left them to it. I told Kerry when I got in, and the general consensus was, now what!

We didn't have to wait long to find out when a week later a letter turned up in our post box. The letter was postmarked with the stamp of Vannes, the administrative headquarters of Morbihan, our department. Hesitantly Kerry opened the envelope and read the letter. It made for grim reading, apparently someone from the 'river police,' just happened to be passing by and noticed our lake. And further investigations revealed that the lake had never been registered, therefore legally didn't exist, so could we fill it in, please! That's what the farmer and clip board man were up to.

We sought advice from our French friends, who told us we should go back to the Notaire and show him the letter. After all we paid for a lake, and a lake is what we should have. And how has this not been found in any legal searches. We made an appointment and went to see him. We showed him the letter, he read it but didn't seem to be impressed. We asked what he was going to do, and he said "Nothing."

We asked what we could do, he gave the gallic shrug and pointed to a filing cabinet,
"See that filing cabinet" he said, "Its full of English clients, that have had property problems."
If this was supposed to make us feel better, it didn't.

We went back to our French friends and told them about our meeting with the Notaire. They couldn't believe his attitude and what he had said. They told us not to worry, and that they would help.

Months of back and forth to the Notaires office was achieving nothing, until on one visit we told him this was pointless, who is your boss, who can we take it higher to. Believing we wouldn't be able to carry it through, and almost daring us. He said, "You can always take your problem with me to the Chambre de Notaires du Morbihan (a sort of ombudsman for solicitors in our department of Morbihan). He even gave us the address; I think he believed we wouldn't do it or even be capable of it. However, he hadn't banked on Kerrys tenacity, she worked diligently on a letter, got French friends to check it over until she was happy with the result, and sent it on. The Chambre de Notaires acknowledged receipt of the letter and said they would look into it. Fearing that meant they wouldn't do anything really, we were surprised when we received a letter from them saying, basically we have been messed about, and they have recommended that the Notaire compensates us to the tune of 1500 euros. Thinking this is probably the best we are going to get out of this, we accepted. We had paid 4000 euros for the lake, so we had got nearly half of it back. On the day we met the Notaire to pick up the cheque, we asked what we should do now. He told us, just do what the French would do, keep your heads down for a couple of years, ignore the letter and just carry on. Great advice from a solicitor.

While we were dealing with the Notaire, we also paid a visit to the Marie, to see if he could offer any help or advice. We went to the reception and asked if we could make an appointment to see the Marie. The receptionist told us.
"No need, he is available now."
We followed the receptionists directions, up the stairs and along the corridor and soon found ourselves knocking on a large oak door.
"Entrez" said a voice, and we went in. The room was a large wood panelled room, with the portraits of every Marie whoever ruled over Guilliers, looking down at proceedings. The Marie was sitting behind a large desk, we approached him and were asked to sit down. He seemed a bit peeved, probably something to do with us disturbing him reading his newspaper, that was spread out on the desk. We told him the story of what had happened to us, regarding the lake and showed him the letter. He read it, looked up and said, "There is nothing I can do" and the way he said it, I thought he was going to add, not that I give a toss. We got up to go and thanked him for seeing us, but he didn't seem to hear or weren't bothered, as he was already back into reading his paper.

We took the Notaires advice and ignored the letter. We carried on with the stump clearing, the tree felling and more often than not, pulling a fallen tree out of the lake. Many times, I got a soaking while going through this process, of pulling a tree out. Sometimes the tree was too big to just pull out, so I had to go in and using my chainsaw cut it into manageable pieces. One time after doing some cuts, I was making my way back to bankside, now I don't know if this was deliberate or not, but Kerry pulled on the rope that was tied around the tree and over I went, totally underwater. And if that wasn't bad enough, I was holding my chainsaw, it was chugging away on tick over, but obviously cut out as it went under water. I made it to the bank, swearing a bit. Amazingly, after a few pulls on the starter rope, the chainsaw started, none the worse for its brief swim. This was when Kerry allowed herself a brief chuckle.

We used to dread letters from the Marie, as it usually meant they weren't happy with a rogue tree on the perimeter, that they thought was unsafe. So could we cut it down or else. Or it would be asking us to cut back the large conifer hedge that ran alongside the lane, just in case a bus went down there.

Up to the present, and during the sale process, the lake not being registered reared its ugly head again. Some research discovered that the lake had been there about 200 years, and in its present form about 100 years. But never registered! The River Police got involved again, and still maintained, despite how long it had been there and how much it would devastate the nature and wildlife at the lake, it had to be returned to how it was before the lake existed. How they can prove that is anybody's guess. I still find it hard to believe they adopted this stance when you consider the environmental impact filling it in would have. All the creatures that called the lake home, as well as the passing visitors like the kingfishers, ducks, and herons. Unbelievable!

Thinking this would scare our buyers off, we expected the worse and that we would be left with a massive problem. There was a slight negotiation with the price and the sale went ahead. Will they do as instructed and fill it in, to reinstate it to its former 200-year self, or is it their turn to ignore the letter!

Chapter Fourteen

In my experience, I found the Breton folk to be such a laid back, chilled out friendly people. So, I could never understand why, that when they got behind the wheel of a car, they turned into some impatient speed freak maniac. They rewrote the common-sense highway code, for overtaking on bends, brow of hills, junctions, they were all fair game for carrying out this manoeuvre. One time I slowed down from 80km/h to 50km/h in obeyance of the road signs, the road narrowed as I passed through a small hamlet. I nearly had cause to wet myself, as a massive truck overtook me and gave me the full blast of its horns. I was unaware speed limits didn't apply to trucks.

On the school run one afternoon, a journey of about 10 km, on a reasonably straight road but with many hills. As I drove down one of these hills, I was overtaken, nothing strange there. But in the opposite direction coming towards me was a car, being overtaken by another impatient driver. My mind quickly evaluated the situation. There was me in my car, with a car heading towards me, and there was a car overtaking me, with a car hurtling towards them. The distance between us was about 500 metres or so, and we must have been travelling at a speed of at least 70km/h. Bugger! I said to myself and probably shut my eyes and braced for impact. But nothing happened, we somehow missed each other and carried on our way.

As we pulled off our drive and onto the single-track lane, if we went left down the hill, we would soon pick up the main road to Guilliers. If we turned right and went up the hill, this would take us immediately between two houses, and here the lane narrowed even more. Just passed the houses, the lane also had a slight bend creating a blind spot. This all added up to making pulling off our drive a tricky manoeuvre, although traffic coming through was rare and anything that did, slowed down to negotiate the gap between the houses. Well, most drivers did, but there are always them special people.

We became aware of one such idiot, when we were sitting in the front garden this particular evening. A car came tearing down the hill and between the two houses at quite a speed, no consideration given to the obvious hazards. If we had been edging off our drive, we would have had no chance, as there was no way that car could have stopped. The next night at around the same time, there it was again, the same car at the same speed. This carried on all week. Fearing a bad accident, we thought we must do something. I had been thinking about making some signs up and putting them up the hill. I had got the idea when driving through another hamlet, and had seen these colourful handmade signs, saying "Ralentir Enfants" which meant "Slow down, Children." Up the lane, there had been an official warning sign but that had gone rusty and fell into the ditch. We had gone to the Marie about getting a new one but were given the standard gallic shrug and a polite "Non." The arrival of this regular speed demon prompted me into action. I knocked up a couple of signs, painted them bright yellow with red lettering and placed them up the hill. The next evening, we waited to see if they would have the desired effect. But no, down the road came Lewis Hamilton, same speed as usual. We gave him the benefit of the doubt, perhaps he hadn't seen the signs; we'll give him a few days before we come up with another plan.

A week later, he still showed no sign of slowing down. Fearful of there being a bad accident and someone being badly hurt, we needed to up our game. One of the boys did suggest a homemade stinger but that idea was quickly dismissed. It was decided we would wait for him, try and flag him down and have a word with him, hopefully explaining our concerns. The next night we laid in wait for him, up the hill away from the houses. And at the same time as usual, he come belting along the lane, foot to the floor and stereo blaring. Between us we did manage to slow him down and get him to stop. Kerry approached the driver's side and obligingly the window came down, but the stereo stayed on. Kerry gave the driver – a lad in his early twenties, a good old fashioned bollocking in her best French. She told him, it wasn't a motorway, there were blind drive exits, children playing, old people using the communal bins and pets. He was driving dangerously and could end up killing someone. Kerrys rant over, she waited for his response. The young man paused, adjusted his sunglasses, and then blew Kerry a kiss. He then rammed the gear stick into first and sped off. Leaving Kerry standing there in a cloud of dust. "Cheeky sod" she shouted, reverting back to Anglo-Saxon.

Despite his cocky reaction, we never saw him again, the streets of Treblou were safe once more. Kerrys little chat must have done the trick.

They have this little car in Brittany called a Sans Permit, it may be available all over France, I'm not sure. Sans Permit means without permit so you can drive one without a driving licence. I was to learn that these were available to people, who had had their licence taken away, for traffic offences, including drink driving. This was because the infrastructure in Brittany was limited if it existed at all. Getting around by bus and train wasn't really an option. The Sans Permit cars had a single cylinder and were capable of a top speed of 30km/h. They were favoured by the convicted drink driving community, you could tell their cars as they had scratches and dents all over them. Despite a top speed of 30km/h they still bumped into things. The typical Sans Permit was a dull grey colour, but we did come across a display of these cars in a local supermarket. There were all different colours and styles including a cabriolet and a van. It was like a toy van with only room for a few tools. They were like little dodgem cars, but they lost their cuteness when you come up behind one of them, doing their top speed along a narrow winding country lane.

One episode worthy of mention in this chapter happened on one of our trips down to France, a short time after we had moved back to the UK. Jacks scooter had been sitting in the garage collecting dust, so he decided he would like to sell it before it started to deteriorate. We popped into our local moto-culture shop, this was a family run business, and we had become friendly with them, after many visits to buy garden machinery and to have the same, serviced and repaired. They sold most types of petrol driven garden equipment, from strimmer's to sit-on mowers, they also sold bicycles and lower range motorbikes like mopeds and scooters. We told them about Jacks scooter and that we were wondering if they would mind putting it on display, at the shop, with a view to selling it. This they agreed to if they could put a small commission on for themselves. The deal done, we shook hands and said we would return with it in the next couple of days.

Back at the house, we gave the scooter a good clean, made sure it started ok and checked the fluid levels. Happy with our work we decided we would take it to the shop the next day. I would ride the scooter, and Kerry would follow in the car. That evening we had been invited round Eddie and Tanya's house for dinner and drinks. We had not seen each other for a while, so we had plenty to talk about, which in turn made us very thirsty. Well, I was, Kerry was designated driver and much to her delight we got home around two in the morning.

I woke up feeling a bit fuzzy headed but nothing a big fry up wouldn't cure. Kerry stepped up and provided an ample breakfast of eggs, bacon, tomatoes, mushrooms, beans, and plenty of toast. Stomachs more than satisfied, we made our plans to take the scooter to the shop. It turns out it wasn't the hardest plan to make, I would set off first and Kerry would follow in the car a few minutes later, so hopefully we would arrive at the shop at around the same time. I started the scooter up and set off. The journey was a distance of about 10 km, I wasn't expecting to encounter much traffic, in fact I wasn't expecting to see another vehicle until I got nearer the town where the shop was. As expected, I had the road to myself, and rode along at a steady speed, imagining I was Sting in Quadrophenia on my way to Brighton, to have a dust up with the Rockers. I was shaken back to reality, when as I neared the shop, I saw two motorcycle cops parked up a couple of hundred metres in front of me. Being near to the shop, I carried on my way. Seeing me coming, which wasn't hard really as I was the only vehicle about, one of them stepped into the road and waved me down. I came to a halt and was motioned at to turn the engine off. The cop then went off like some

verbal machine gun, not understanding any of it, I put my hand up and in my best French said,
"Sorry, I am English, I don't understand."
In response I got a terse "So!"
"Bloody hell" I thought, this could be bad. I looked down the road hoping to see Kerry, but there was no sign of her. I managed to understand that they wanted to see my driving licence, which I gave to them. They gave it the once over, they seemed happy with it and gave it back. Brexit hadn't happened yet and wasn't round to complicate things when it came to driving French registered vehicles. I was then asked for my insurance, oh shit! I hadn't given it a thought, but then again, I didn't expect to be pulled over by the cops. And so close to the shop, I had nearly made it. I tried to explain that the scooter was my sons, and I didn't know where he had put it. It is normal in France, to have your insurance certificate, a green piece of paper put in a plastic sleeve and stuck to the vehicle. In a car it would be stuck to the windscreen so you could see at once that you were insured. We looked over the scooter, and just when I was detecting a mood of happiness coming over the cops, realising they had got me for a traffic offence, we found it! A massive sense of relief washed over me. But this feeling was short lived, it had run out – two days ago! The cops faces saddened by finding the certificate, lit up again. I could almost hear them saying,
"Got him, got the English pig dog."
Things moved on from being serious to being very serious, they even became a tad aggressive. They were talking away, but I had no idea what they were going on about. Thankfully, it was at this point that Kerry pulled up. She got out of the car and marched over; I gave her a worried look.
Getting straight into French and explaining who she was, she asked the cops, what was going on. They told her I

had been caught driving without insurance and they would need a statement. Also, I would have to be breathalysed, Kerry passed this information on to me. "Bugger!" I thought, remembering the gallon of beer and wine I had put away the previous evening. I'm going to spend the night in a French prison. The breathalyser was produced, and I blew into it as instructed. There was an agonised wait, and I gave Kerry a concerned look, I say concerned, it was more of a I'm shitting myself kind of a look. At last, the cop staring at the breathalyser, looked up and almost disappointedly said,
"Negative"
That surge of relief flooded through me again. Now just the problem of no insurance to deal with. Kerry gave all the required details for the statement; it seemed to go on for ages. When she got to the bit about taking it to the moto culture shop to sell it, I noticed a shift in their mood, almost an air of "have we been wasting our time." They said they needed to check with the shop, so over the road we marched and went in. We were greeted by the manager, he seemed to throw Kerry and myself, a don't worry sort of look. The manager and the police had a semi heated discussion, the managers tone and body language suggested there was no love lost here. The discussion went on for about ten minutes or so, when suddenly the cops wheeled round, and made to leave the shop, passing by us, one of them turned to Kerry and said, "You will be hearing from us." They crossed the road, got on their motorbikes, and sped off.

With them out of the way, the manager told us of his dislike and distrust for the Gendarmes, especially the motorcycle variety. He explained that he had told them, because we were bringing the scooter to his shop, for him to sell it, that it would be covered on his insurance. He told us not to worry everything will be fine. We thanked him, shook hands, and said our goodbyes. I wasn't convinced, I had the distinct feeling that those cops didn't go a lot on the English and would not let it go.

A couple of weeks later we had an email from the shop – good news. They had sold Jacks scooter, and them two cops had come back to the shop to see if the scooter was actually up for sale. Seeing it was, they had told the manager that they wouldn't be taking any further action. That feeling of relief surged through my body once again. I was not guilty, I was free – no guillotine, no French penal colony, on some distant remote island, or whatever the French judiciary would have served up to a wayward Englishman.

Before I leave road users, one character who deserves a mention is the old boy who used to cycle into Guilliers every morning for his baguette and bottle of wine. We would often see him on the main road, he would be cycling so slow we were surprised he wasn't going backwards. He was travelling that slow; by staying upright he seemed to defy the laws of gravity. He came up in conversation with a friend, who told us that he lived in her hamlet and did the trip twice a day, once in the morning, once in the afternoon, both times to pick up a baguette and a bottle of wine.

Chapter Fifteen

As this book nears its end, I have given this chapter over to small bitesize chunks of stories, that happened to us or our friends, during our six years of living in France.

A friend of ours, Jeff, was a keen royalist and took it bad when the Queens Mother died in 2002. On the day of the funeral, he sat glued to the TV drowning his sorrows with vast quantities of wine. As the event progressed, and fuelled by the wine, he thought it would be a good idea to offer up his own tribute. He took his shotgun out of its cabinet, grabbed some cartridges, and went out into the garden. Firing the gun in the air, he carried out his own version of a 21-gun salute. As the last shots echo faded away, satisfied with his work, he returned to his armchair. About half an hour later, he thought he saw a figure sneaking around his garden. Paying close attention to his garden now, he noticed another figure, and another and then another. What's going on out there? he thought and made his way to the door. Standing at the door, he shouted,
"Who's there, what's going on."
Seeing he was unarmed, several SWAT type police all stood up from their various hiding places in the bushes and shrubs. He noticed how they were all dressed in black uniforms with matching helmets, and they were armed with assault rifles, and they were all pointing at him.
"Whoa" he shouted, and quickly put his hands up.
The squad moved slowly in his direction, with their rifles still trained on him, and the Officer in charge started barking instructions.
"Don't shoot, don't shoot" Jeff spluttered, "I don't understand, I'm English."

Luckily for him one of the police spoke good English,
"What's going on, there's been reports of gunshots fired, is everyone ok," said the cop.
"Oh, bloody hell" said Jeff, and hastily explained what he had been up to.
He could see the squad visibly relax, and Jeff felt a bit better and realised he had never sobered up so quickly.
The English-speaking Cop said,
"We will need to check the house over, if that's ok."
Who was going to argue?
The house given the once over and noticing the funeral ceremony on the telly, the squad proper relaxed and stood down. They even saw the funny side of it now. Jeff heard that a neighbour, hearing multiple gunshots and fearing the worst, especially as it was close season for hunting, had called it in. As the squad left, one of the police officers who hadn't spoken any English up to now, turned to Jeff and said,
"You English, you are crazy."
And with that they were gone.

Harry recalls a time, when a travelling fair turned up in Mauron, and he and a group of pals were out enjoying the rides. They were on the dodgems, when a row kicked off between the guy running the ride and a local lad. As the row escalated to pushing and shoving, the fairground guy ran to his kiosk, emerged with a shotgun, and started randomly shooting up the town square. Everyone dived for cover including Harry and his mates. But before any harm could be done, the Gendarmes were soon on the scene. Lots of them with lots of guns. The fair ground shooter realising the game was up, dropped his gun and quickly surrendered. The only damage was some pellet holes in the side of a building and a few branches and leaves blown from a nearby tree. Never a dull moment in the sleepy French countryside.

Throughout the summer, there was always mini festivals happening in the local towns and villages. As always there would be food and drink, and of course live music. As a rule, the bands were pretty awful, despite this they were always good nights out. There were a couple of exceptional music nights out though. One day we were driving down an auto route and there by the side of the road, was a massive billboard advertising, Status Quo, appearing at Nantes. At our local Leclerc supermarket, it had been noticed before that they had a desk there, that advertised selling excursions, theatre, and concert tickets. We made a point of going there and asked about the Quo tickets, yes, they had some and they were 30 euros each. What a bargain. I had been a Quo fan since I was a teenager, seeing my first concert in the seventies at Hammersmith Odeon, as it was then. The family had never had the pleasure, but it didn't take me long to talk them into going. Concert day arrived and we made the two-hour drive down to Nantes. We found the concert venue with ease and there was a massive car park, so parking wasn't a problem either. We took our seats, and I couldn't help but notice that this wasn't the usual denim clad Quo crowd I was used to. In fact, they were all very smart, dressed in their finery looking more like they were going to the opera. There wasn't a great deal of headbanging, the atmosphere was a touch muted, but the Quo gave us a great show. Well, I thought so.

We were also lucky to see The Fratellis and Razorlight one night, at a mini festival. We happened to notice a poster at that ticket counter in Leclercs, advertising a mini festival with Razorlight headlining. There were four other bands, the Fratellis, another obscure English band and two French bands that I hadn't heard of, but the boys were vaguely aware off. The festival was on a Friday night at St. Brieuc, which was about a two hours' drive from us. Tickets were twenty-five euros each, we all liked Razorlight and the Fratellis, it seemed like a bargain. Come the day, we picked the kids up from school and made our way up to St Brieuc. The town was heaving when we got there but we managed to find a parking space and made our way to the venue. We followed the signs to what looked like a massive supermarket carpark, with a rather large marquee, set up on it. We grabbed a programme and were pleased to see that The Fratellis were second band on and Razorlight were due to appear at 22.30. One of the French bands were on last, with the festival due to finish at 2 AM, at least we wouldn't have to suffer them and could start the long journey home after Razorlight had finished. The first band on, were the English band that we hadn't heard of. They were a bit of a cheesy cliché band, the lead singer did the full repertoire, of swinging the mike around and skipping with the mike lead, although he did fall over, while doing this. He did attempt to crowd surf, as he leapt from the stage, the crowd parted leaving him floundering on the floor.

Watching this first act, along with us was an audience of about two hundred people. And this stayed the same for the Fratellis, who were quite popular in the UK at this time, with a string of big hits. They played a good set and were quite brilliant but deserved a bigger crowd.

As the time of Razorlights appearance got closer, the place started to fill up and was proper rammed when they came on stage. It would appear that most people had only come to see them. Like The Fratellis they played a good show, and we had a great time. But as they departed so did we. We were at home and in bed by 3 AM, the kids first taste of rock and roll.

A summer activity that we all embraced, was camping. Although Jack didn't take to using the toilet facilities on site, and somehow his bodies digestive system shut down until we got home. As mentioned before, we had camped down the lake a few times and had been under canvas while on a few cricket tours. We also did a week in Normandy, staying on a lovely little campsite near the D-Day landings area. For me it was a giant history lesson. We explored the beaches, the museums, the cemeteries, and memorials. We also took a trip into Bayeaux to see the Tapestry, although the kids were more impressed by the campsites swimming pool. And Harry had a particular fascination with the site toilets, there were a row of 20 'traps'. Unlike Jacks constitution I'm sure Harry used all of them.

But the camping holiday that has gone down in our family folk lore was our week on the Ile d'Oleron. This is an island off the west coast of France, joined to the mainland by a 3 km bridge. We had heard that the Island was extremely popular with the French, so it must be good. We found a campsite we liked the look of and booked a pitch. The day we drove down, what should have been a four-hour journey took us a couple of hours more, as a storm had blown in and the driving conditions were terrible. We did even think of turning round and going home at one point. We persevered and arrived at the campsite; the weather conditions had changed – it was worse. Needing somewhere to sleep that night, we put the tent up, in what felt like a force 9 storm. This was made doubly tricky by the fact it was a new tent. This new purchase was a massive four roomed dome tent, basically a big dome – the living area, and four bedrooms attached to this. And it was dark! How we managed it, I will never know, but we managed to set it up, albeit with a lot of swearing. The boys helped out valiantly, while

Maggie sheltered in the car. Tent set up; we could get out of our wet clothes. While the kids snuggled into their beds, Kerry and I fell into a bottle of wine.

Waking up to a quieter day, sticking my head out of the tent there was quite a bit of storm damage. Branches down and general debris everywhere. I noticed two pitches along, was a family with their bags packed and what was left of their tent sticking out of a wheelie bin. We had been lucky.

The storm had passed, and the sun had come out, so we set off to do our first day of exploring. The Island seemed pleasant enough, but it felt a little tired, like it could do with a bit of TLC, a general tidy up and a lick of paint. Our first meal at a restaurant revealed the Islands speciality, 'moules frites' – mussels and chips. The menu consisted mostly of moules frites with different sauces. I wasn't fazed, I love moules frites as do the kids. Kerry on the other hand wasn't a fan and had an omelette. And that was pretty much our staple diet for the week, it didn't matter what restaurant we went into, the menu was the same.

Back at the tent, and the first night of sleep without storm Edna raging outside, brought to our attention that there was a lighthouse nearby. This becomes apparent, as the searchlight scanned the campsite about every ten seconds, giving us that second world war prisoner of war camp experience.

For our daytime activities, the beaches were pleasant enough, but the weather wasn't exactly beach weather. There were crazy golf courses everywhere, so we played that every day, sometimes twice. We found a fair that looked like it was a travelling fair, which had pitched up about 25 years ago and had never moved on. Like the rest of the Island, it looked like it could do with a clean-up and a lick of paint. It was supposed to open at 5 PM, so we got there one evening at 6 PM, but nothing was happening. We had parked nearby, so went and sat back in the car. There were two other cars parked up, with eager families looking on expectantly. Just as we were at the point of giving up, the door of a caravan parked up behind the fair, opened up and a man walked towards one of the rides. He started the ride up, it was like a rubbish waltzer and to make it look even worse, most of the bulbs festooned around the ride didn't work. I'm not a fan of this kind of ride, so I made my excuses saying I would take some photos and let the rest of them get on. When the ride had finished, Kerry asked if any of the other rides would be opening. When I say other rides, there were only three others. The feller running the waltzer gave an abrupt "Non" and walked back to his caravan. Oh well, so much for a night at the fair.

The only other attraction that sticks in the memory was a Ragondin or Coypu, petting zoo. Desperately trying to entertain ourselves we gave it a go. When we paid our admission fee, for an extra euro we could buy a bag of sliced carrots to feed the coypu. Sod the expense, we had a bag each. The zoo such as it was, consisted of three concrete circular pens, in each were about a dozen or so of these creatures. This wasn't going to keep us occupied for very long. After walking around the pens for the third time, things livened up, when one of the keepers told us that Maggie could go into one of the pens and feed the coypus by hand. Despite her protests I lifted Maggie into one of the pens. Thankfully, she wasn't attacked, and the coypu were much more interested in the carrots. They ate greedily and at least they were happy, unlike Maggie who was totally unimpressed.

As a footnote, one of the reasons for choosing the Ile d'Oleron was that the French refer to this place as the Island of Light, because its notable for its quality of light – it rained every day!

Back home and one wine fuelled evening with Eddie and Tanya, we hatched a plan for a day out. It was decided that Jack, Harry, and me, plus Eddie and Dennis would go out on a day's adventure. The idea was that we would all be blindfolded, and then driven about 10 to 15 kms away and dropped off. We would have to use all our skills and cunning to find our way home. As the day neared, it was decided that Eddie and I wouldn't be blindfolded, we were to leave the challenge to the boys, to unravel but could offer guidance, so we didn't end up walking in totally the wrong direction or any other nonsense. To add to the intrigue the boys wouldn't know that we hadn't been blindfolded. Left to their own devices, albeit with a little nudging from the adults, the boys managed to get us back home in about six hours. The boys reward for this achievement was to watch the movie, Blair Witch, sitting in the woods. A massive extension lead was run into the woods to provide power for a TV and DVD player. And fair play to the boys, they sat there in the woods as the sun set and darkness arrived and watched the whole film.

When questioned if he had been scared, Harry said,
"Not really, the ghost in my bedroom was scarier."
"Eh! What happened" I said.
"I was asleep, and Monty was lying on the bed with me, I was woken up by Monty making a strange growling sound, not the sort of noise you expect a cat to make. And there was a beige coloured man standing there, he had a suit on and was wearing a top hat. He walked across the room and through the wall into Jacks

bedroom. And with that, Monty legged it, and I must have fallen back to sleep."

The weather in our part of Brittany was pretty standard. The summers were usually nice, with temperatures a few degrees hotter than where we lived in Kent. The winters were grey, foggy, and wet. But there are two weather events worthy of a mention. The first happened one hot and sunny summers afternoon. We were at a friend's house for a barbecue, as his village was holding a fete and a road cycling race, that was going right past his house. The fete was held in the village square and basically consisted of several food and drink stalls. The cycle race was several laps of the surrounding countryside including the main road through the village. There was a good turnout, as you would expect in France, with a mixture of food, booze and cycling to enjoy. People had set up camp alongside the road and were enjoying their picnic and the race. The weather had been superb. When all of a sudden out of nowhere, the sky, darkened almost like night-time, a strong wind blew up and the sky unleashed a mighty hailstorm. We all dashed under a gazebo that up and till now had been used as a shade from the heat of the sun. The gazebo bent and buckled under the storm, and with two people holding a pole at each corner, this was managing to provide us with some shelter. I noticed that our car parked nearby had its windows open, I grabbed the keys and made a dash for it. I jumped into the car and shut the windows. As I sat there, the hailstones increased in size and intensity, the noise of them bouncing off the car was almost unbearable. Just as I thought I couldn't stand it anymore, as quick as the storm arrived, it was gone. I got out of the car and couldn't help but notice the dents on the bonnet and roof, the hailstones had been the size of golf balls. The gazebo had just about managed to stay

standing although it had a few new ventilation holes in it. It was at this point that Kerry said.
"The roof windows at home are all open, and the tent is set up in the garden."
Home was only a short drive away, so fearing the worse I set off to make sure everything was ok. As I headed off along the main road, there were upturned tables and chairs where spectators had once been. The fete in the village square was now a pile of canvas, metal framework and other debris forced into one corner. A tall pine tree that stood alongside the church, and that had up until a few minutes ago towered over the steeple, had been snapped in half. I carried on to our place dreading what I was going to find. At about two minutes from home, I noticed there was no hailstones melting by the side of the road and the roads weren't even wet. Arriving at home, all was good, no damage, no sign the storm had even been there.

The other weather event took place in the depths of winter. I remember letting Frolly out for a pee, this particular night at about 11 PM, nothing out of the ordinary there, just your average chilly winters night. Off to bed and after a night's sleep the alarm woke me up at 6.30 AM. I crossed the bedroom floor to the walk-in cupboard and as I passed by the window, I was stopped in my tracks. It had been snowing and quite a lot of snow too, there must be about two foot of the stuff laying out there, and it was still snowing. Turning back to the bed I said to Kerry,
"Well, that's that then, back to bed for me, I'm not going anywhere, there's a couple of foot of snow laying out there and it's still coming down."

Now normally wild horses couldn't drag the kids out of bed on a school day, but no sooner had I snuggled back

into bed and having heard what I said, all three of them were in our bedroom staring out of the window planning their day.
"Get back to bed" I shouted.
But five minutes later they were downstairs with hats and scarves on, eating their breakfast. After a short while, I went downstairs and opened the front door, the snow was up to the door handle. Frolly desperate for his morning constitution, took a flying leap and disappeared into the snow drift, I reached over and dragged him out by his collar. I needed to clear an area around the front door so Frolly could go out, and where was Monty? I struggled over to the shed to get my snow shovel, and as I started clearing an area the words of a French pal came into my head. Standing in my shed one afternoon, he noticed the large snow shovel hanging up and asked me what I used it for. When I told him, he said "you won't have any use for that, it never snows here."

Later on, that morning and having nothing better to do, we asked our neighbours if they needed any bread from the village as we were going to attempt to walk there. Normally it takes us half an hour to walk into Guilliers, in these conditions it took us over two hours. When we got to the village, it had a nice feel to it, there was the smell of freshly cooked bread hanging in the cold air, mixing with the smell of strong coffee coming from the Tabac. There were pockets of people standing around chatting and laughing and talking about the weather, it was like a scene from a Dickens novel. Arriving back home, we were pleased to see Monty sitting by the front door, he didn't look to dishevelled, who knows where he had been hiding or how he had made his way to the door.

It was three days before the road into Treblou was cleared and that only happened because a local farmer pushed his way through in his tractor. It was a week before things got back to something like normality. However, the massive snowman the kids had built on the bend at the top of the hill was reluctant to melt and was used as a roundabout for a couple of weeks.

One of Jacks hobbies, considered macabre by some, was collecting animal skulls. He had always had an interest in fossils. But I think the skull thing started, when he found a rather large, dead pike on the bank of Bewl Water reservoir, which is situated on the Kent and Sussex border. He wanted to take it home, so it could be boiled, cleaned up, and then the plan was, that he could put the head or jaws on display. It was rather smelly and there was no way it was going in the car. But following Jacks insistence, it was put in a bag and tied onto the cycle rack, at the back of the car. It survived the journey home, and Jack set about cleaning it up. It didn't come out as he had hoped but it pricked an interest, which he was able to nurture, when we moved to France. Coming home from a job, one afternoon with Jack and towing the trailer. Seeing a dead badger on the grass verge, he talks me into turning round and picking it up. This is not as easy as it seems, it was going rotten and the smell! lets just say there was a lot of retching and heaving. We managed to get it on the trailer, and once home, it ended up the garden under half a barrel. The maggots did a great job, and Jack soon had his badgers skull, as pride of place in his bedroom. One day, there was a loud banging on the door, and there stood Jack, and in his arms, he held a dead fox! "Well, you're not bringing that in here, take it up the garden." The garden was often full up, with his roadkill finds. He would also, take great delight in finding an owls nest or roost, and would raid it for the little rodent skulls. Boot fairs were also a great source of supply for this bizarre hobby. He bought a cows skull, several deer's including horns, goats and even a dolphin. Not sure about the ethics with this one though, or even how the seller even came to have it.

As this story nears its end, as much as I enjoyed my life in France there were three things that really got up my nose. The first was the traffic regulation of giving way to the right. I could never understand how it was, that you could be driving along a main road, and you were expected to stop to allow a vehicle out from a side road. In reality and in most cases, as two cars approached, one on the main road and one from the side. Both cars would slow down unsure, as to what the other would do, and often both would stop. This was the favourable outcome, but there were many stories of both cars not stopping and a collision taking place, resulting in injuries or worse. Who ever thought this rule up, must have had more than his fair share of wine that day.

The second thing was French radio. To be fair this was a delight we only experienced when driving. Our main car, a Renault Kangoo and Kerry's little sports model, a Renault 5 only had radios and not CD players. In France, the rule is that the radio station must play at least 40% French music. I can understand the sentiment of protecting the French music industry but to meet the figures there was a lot of talentless rubbish played. Also, the radio stations weren't allowed to meet this quota by just playing the bigger French 'hits' over and over again. And anyone any good usually sung in English to gain a bigger worldwide audience. So, driving around would mean having to endure 40% of tuneless self-indulgent tripe. This aside, we did get a couple of family 'favourites,' the only one sticks in the brain though and that's because of our trip down to the Il d'Oleron, when this tune was the flavour of the month. The song was called 'And the winner is...' by a guy called Gerard Darman. He warbled away in French for almost all the song but sang the title in English. Which of course we all joined in with. The best of it is, when we are over in France now, all these years later, the same dreadful songs are still on the radio.

The third thing on this short list that I disliked, no hated with a passion was the hunt, 'Le Chasse.' I've never been one of those people that has been into killing animals for fun, sport or whatever, but your average French hunter, was a rude arrogant asshole and after lunch, he became a drunk, rude, arrogant asshole. The Breton countryside, with its forests, rivers and streams and wide-open spaces is a beautiful place for a stroll, but come September everything changes. The hunting season starts in September and finishes around the end of February, the worst days are Sundays and Thursdays, but any day of the week can be a problem. Any outdoor pursuit such as dog walking or cycling becomes a life-or-death experience and wearing bright clothing or a Hi-Viz becomes a necessity. It is a regulation that all hunters should wear a Hi-Viz cap and some even follow this rule. This was bought in because, as well as shooting animals, passers-by and just about anything that moves, they are also quite good at shooting each other. I read somewhere that on average in France, about forty hunters a year are shot by other hunters, some fatally. They are not supposed to shoot towards a road, but they do, as Eddie and I found out one morning. We were cycling along a lane between some trees, when we came out from the cover, there walking across the field towards the road was a row of hunters. As we spotted them, a pheasant chose this time to leave his hidey hole on the ground and take to the air between us and the hunters. The hunters raised their guns and fired. I'm not sure it would have made any difference but we both ducked and tried to take evasive action. Thankfully, we weren't hit, neither was the pheasant, who flew off into the nearby woods. Regaining our composure, we gave the hunters some abuse, but not too much, recognising they were armed.

They were not supposed to go within 250 metres of any property and definitely not shoot towards a property, but they did! One Sunday afternoon, the boys come running into the house shouting, "there are hunters at the back and their dogs are in the garden chasing the chickens." If I could digress for a moment, these hunting dogs are kept locked up in pens for six months of the year. The dogs given their freedom run amok. The first day of the season is the worst, the dogs are taken up the woods and let go, excited to have their freedom they run off in all directions. The countryside is awash with hunting dogs living their best life. Back to the hunting dogs in the garden, I ran round to see two dogs hassling the chickens, I shouted and managed to shoo them off. Looking around the garden I noticed one of the chickens lying in a pile of feathers, the dogs had got one. The hunters were stood nearby, just casually watching what was going on. I picked up the dead chicken, held it up and shouted after them. They carried out a group gallic shrug and changed their posture as if to emphasise the fact they were carrying shotguns. They really couldn't have given a damn, and with that they turned round and strolled off. I thought about unleashing a torrent of good old Anglo-Saxon swearwords but decided against it.

One guy who I wasn't so restrained with, was the chief of the local hunt. I had not long left the house, and I was walking up the lane by the woods, with Frolly and Sonny. And as normal the dogs were off the lead, as the chance of a car passing by was remote. However, this particular morning, the sound of a car coming up the lane, had me calling the dogs over, which surprisingly they did. The car stopped and out got this beet faced stroppy looking geezer; my first impression proved to be correct as he let of a shouty tirade of angry French. I didn't get much of it, only that he was the chief of the hunt and walking dogs off their leads was 'interdit,' forbidden. Coming off the back of having a chicken killed in my garden, by off the lead, hunting dogs, I wasn't best pleased. So, in my best French I tried reasoning with him, and then arguing but this made him stroppier, and his face went redder and redder. Just when I thought his head was going to explode, I bought proceedings to an abrupt end by shouting in perfect English "Fuck Off." I think the phrase is pretty universally understood, and if he didn't understand, he got the sentiment and got back in his car and drove off. I thought my outburst could cause me problems as I had been told, at some point previously, do not mess with the hunt especially the chief, they have friends in high places.

Thankfully, I didn't have any fallout from our meeting, in fact the next time I saw him was pretty much the same scenario. I was further along the lane around the bend, dogs off the lead as usual when he went passed. No stopping or English swearword lesson this time, he just kept going but stopping about half a mile further on. I kept an eye on him, he got out of his car, went round the back, and opened the tailgate. He fumbled about in the boot and stood aside, several grouse type birds suddenly flew out of the back and came straight for us. They flew low and just about cleared my head, the dogs both being labradors had their primeval interest pricked and turned around and gave chase. I thought, oh bloody hell, here comes another row.

I looked towards the chief of the hunts car, and he either didn't see or didn't care, and the car pulled away and drove off. I turned my attention to the dogs and set off after them. I rounded a large bramble bush, and came upon them, they had caught one of the birds. I wasn't sure if they had killed it or it had died of shock, there wasn't any marks on the unfortunate creature. I picked it up and took it home, the thinking being, waste not want not, we might as well eat it. By the time its feathers were plucked, it was about the size of a sparrow and would only be good for a very small casserole. The poor bird was consigned to the bin.

If the morning of hunt day was considered risky, the afternoon was considered bloody dangerous. The mornings killing spree usually came to an end around midday, whereupon 'Le chasse' would descend upon a restaurant for food and vast quantities of alcohol. Suitably replenished and over refreshed with pastis and wine, they would take up arms and return to the countryside. Now nothing would be safe from these gangs of drunken fools. We drove up behind one such gang one afternoon, they were walking eight abreast across the road, shotguns in hand. They walked with a swagger that suggested they were on their way to the OK corral rather than looking for some defenceless creature they could blow into pieces.

Chapter Sixteen

This book tells the story of our six years of living in the tiny hamlet of Treblou, in the Brittany countryside. This adventure came to an end in 2008, when circumstances contrived to have us move back to England. Moving back was a tough call, especially for me, but things were happening that made the decision unavoidable. The boys were at that time when they wanted to leave school and wanted the same opportunities that I had had when I was a young man. Treblou was quite remote, great when you're a kid, enjoying all the activities the countryside can give, but not so good when you want to find local work and socialising opportunities. Throw into the mix the credit crunch and financial crisis of this year, which had the world economy on the brink of collapse, causing my work to dry up pretty much overnight. There seemed no other choice but to move back to the UK. Special thanks should be given here for my dad, who gave up his bedroom, moved into his dining room and let us all, including Frolly, stay at his place for ten months until we found our feet. Tough times.

I still look back fondly at those six years in France, despite some tough times, I will always look on them as some of the best years of my life. It was a great adventure and always something I will be proud of that we did as a family. I'll leave the last word to Kerry and as she said on our appearance on the BBC, referring to our life in France,
"Yes, the grass is greener, but boy, do you have to mow it."

FIN

Printed in Great Britain
by Amazon

61237696R00117